THE General WORLDBUILDING GUIDE

Accomplishing Innovation Press

The General Worldbuilding Guide

JM Paquette

Accomplishing Innovation Press

The General Worldbuilding Guide
Copyright © 2023 JM Paquette. All rights reserved.

Accomplishing Innovation Press
1497 Main St. Suite 169
Dunedin, FL 34698
accomplishinginnovationpress.com
AccomplishingInnovationPress@gmail.com

Cover and Typesetting by Autumn Skye
Edited by Accomplishing Innovation Press

All rights to the work within are reserved to the author and publisher. No part of this publication may be reproduced, stored in a retrieval system, or transmitted in any form or by any means, electronic, mechanical, photocopying, recording, scanning, or otherwise, except as permitted under Section 107 or 108 of the 1976 International Copyright Act, without prior written permission except in brief quotations embodied in critical articles and reviews. Please contact either the Publisher or Author to gain permission.

This book is meant as a reference guide. All characters, organizations, and events portrayed in this book are a product of the author. All brands, quotes, and cited work respectfully belong to the original rights holders and bear no affiliation to the authors or publisher.

Library of Congress Control Number: 2022939121

Paperback ISBN-13: 978-1-64450-631-8
Hardcover ISBN-13: 978-1-64450-970-8

Dedication

For all my fellow Pantsers out there!

Table of Contents

Dedication V
Preface XI
Why You Should Trust Me XIII
What is Worldbuilding? XV
How to Use This Book XVII

Part One: In the beginning 1
   A. Creation 2
   A1. Earth-Variant Creation 8
      1. Creation Fun Activity: Mapmaking 10
      2. Alternate Creation Fun Activity 12
      2a. Super-Secret Alternate Fun Activity 13
   B. Gods 16
   B1: Earth-Variant Gods 23
      3. Gods Fun Activity: Pick Your Powers 25
      4. Character Building Activity: Connect the Dots 26
   C. Myths and Legends 28
   C1: Earth-Variant Myths and Legends 31
      5. Myths and Legends Fun Activity: Create Legends, Myths, and Folk Tales! ... 33
   D. I Need a Hero 36
   D1: Earth-Variant Heroes 41
      6. Heroic Fun Activity: Heroes and Villains 43
      7. Character Building Activity: Name Your Characters' Heroes! ... 44

Build Your World Activities 45
      8. Opposites Attract: What is the tension in your world? ... 46
      9. Build a Timeline for your World 48
      10. Your Story Time: In the Beginning 51

Part Two: The world is ... complicated 55

- A. Maps and the Known World 56
- A1. Earth-Variant Maps 60
  - 11. Known World Fun Activity 62
- B. Government 64
- B1. Earth-Variant Government 71
  - 12. Government Fun Activity 73
- C. Society 74
- C1. Earth-Variant Society 78
  - 13. Society Fun Activity 80
- D. Cultural Practices 81
- D1. Earth-Variant Cultural Practices 90
  - 14. Culture Fun Activity 92
- E. Warfare 95
- E1. Earth-Variant Warfare 99
  - 15. Warfare Fun Activity 101
- F. Appearance 103
- F1. Earth-Variant Appearance 107
  - 16. Clothing Fun Activity: Dress Your Characters 109
  - 17. Appearance Fun Activity: Dress Your Side Characters 110

Build Your World Activities 113
- 18. Character Culture Study 114
- 19. FIGHT! 116
- 20. Your Story Time: The World is ... Complicated 120

Part Three: But why did they do that? 123

- A. Economy 124
- A1. Earth-Variant Economy 128
  - 21. Economy Fun Activity 130
- B. Education 131
- B1. Earth-Variant Education 135
  - 22. Education Fun Activity 137
- C. Relationships 139
- C1. Earth-Variant Relationships 148
  - 23. Relationships Fun Activity: What is love? 150
- D. Communication 152
- D1. Earth-Variant Communication 158
  - 24. Communication Fun Activity: I'm sorry, but I don't speak _____. 160
- E. Technology 161
- E1. Earth-Variant Technology 165
  - Technology Fun Activity: Name That Device 167
- F. Travel 168
- F1. Earth-Variant Travel 172

26. Travel Fun Activity: Dream Vacation 174
G. Health and Wellness (Medicine) 175
G1. Earth-Variant Health and Wellness 180
   27. Health and Wellness Fun Activity: Disease 182

Build Your World Activities 185
   28. What is Truth? 186
   29. Motivation and Goals 188
   30. Your Story Time: But why did they do that? 190

Part Four: Mechanics 193
A. Science 194
A1. Earth-Variant Science 198
   31. Science Fun Activity 200
B. Nature 201
B1. Earth-Variant Nature 204
   32. Nature Fun Activity: Name that plant! 206
C. Weather 207
C1. Earth-Variant Weather 210
   33. Weather Fun Activity 212
D. Measuring Time, Distance, and Weight 213
   34. Measurements Fun Activity: Vocabulary Time 216
   35. Measurement Fun Activity: Calendar Time 217

Build Your World Activities 219
   36. It's Science! 220
   37. It's perfectly natural 221
   38. Like the weather 222
   39. Measure me! 223
   40. Your Story Time: Mechanics 224

Part Five: Who lives in your world? 227
A. People 228
A1. Earth-Variant People 233
   41. People Fun Activity: The World at a Glance 235
   42. Fight Club 238
   43. Traditional or Progressive? Fun Activity 239
B. Creatures 240
B1. Earth-Variant Creatures 246
   44. Creature Fun Activity 248
   45. I once had a 250

Build Your World Activities 251
   46. Ancestry Time 252
   47. When did that start? 256

48. Eagles over Pigeons, hands down. 257
49. How to hunt a bear ... in winter. 258
50. Your Story Time: Who lives in your world? 259

Part Six: Useful Stuff 261
A. Character Card: Describe your characters all in one place! 262
B. Plot Points: Keep it Straight. 268
C. Story Profile Time 274
D. Top Five Time 276

References mentioned in this book 282

Preface

I love reading. Nothing gives me more joy than jumping into a new story, meeting new characters, seeing people and places through another set of eyes, and immersing myself in a different world. A good story has more than great characters and clever dialogue, though. A great story is housed within a believable secondary universe. Without a well-developed world to support people and conversations, a story will feel thin somehow—incomplete, an echo of something that could be earth-shattering but ends up merely yawn-worthy.

Building a coherent world for a story can seem like complicated stuff, and sometimes the details get lost in the shuffle of creating the plot, the characters, the dialogue, the goal/motivation/conflict trifecta—all the complex planning that goes into writing.

Don't worry! This book is here to help!

As a writer, I like to think I know all about the world my characters inhabit. But do I? I will get hung up on a scene because I haven't yet thought about the underlying assumptions of a minor character, the subtle dynamics lying beneath the surface of an interaction at the bar, or the historical relationship between different cultures. Then, I get stuck because I have to stop and puzzle out the details I could have planned way before my characters got to that point. The more I know about my world, the better I can focus on the story while maintaining a coherent background.

But what sort of things should I know about my world beyond my story and my characters?

That's where this book comes in.

In the following chapters, you'll find questions and exercises designed to help you iron out the details of your world. Some of them are obvious: what are the different cultures in your world? Do they get along? Who is in charge?

Some of them are not-so-obvious: what are the historical interactions that led to the current relationships? Why did things work out the way they did? How much history do your characters know?

A comedian once explained how he would never cheat on his wife because he had worked out the possible scenarios in his mind beforehand and decided how he would behave if the situation should present itself.[1] Consider this book your chance to have all sorts of conversations with your characters so that when they are in a situation, you won't have to stop to work out the world mechanics—you will already know! Many of the answers you create will not explicitly feature in your story but knowing them in the back of your mind will make the story you write more believable.

---

[1] The joke, of course, was that he had never had that conversation with himself about robbing a train (Bert Kreischer: The Machine!).

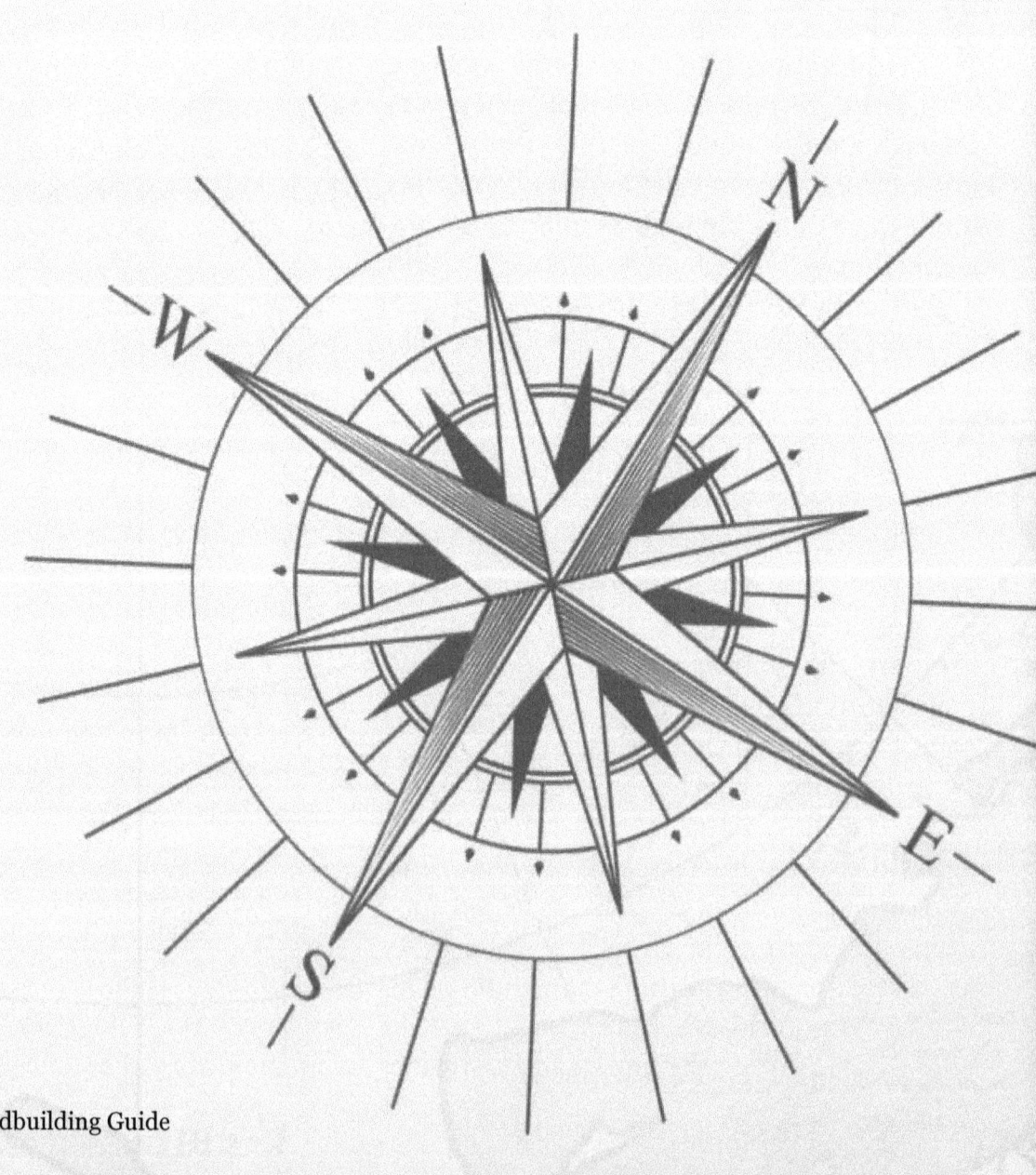

Preface

I love reading. Nothing gives me more joy than jumping into a new story, meeting new characters, seeing people and places through another set of eyes, and immersing myself in a different world. A good story has more than great characters and clever dialogue, though. A great story is housed within a believable secondary universe. Without a well-developed world to support people and conversations, a story will feel thin somehow—incomplete, an echo of something that could be earth-shattering but ends up merely yawn-worthy.

Building a coherent world for a story can seem like complicated stuff, and sometimes the details get lost in the shuffle of creating the plot, the characters, the dialogue, the goal/motivation/conflict trifecta—all the complex planning that goes into writing.

Don't worry! This book is here to help!

As a writer, I like to think I know all about the world my characters inhabit. But do I? I will get hung up on a scene because I haven't yet thought about the underlying assumptions of a minor character, the subtle dynamics lying beneath the surface of an interaction at the bar, or the historical relationship between different cultures. Then, I get stuck because I have to stop and puzzle out the details I could have planned way before my characters got to that point. The more I know about my world, the better I can focus on the story while maintaining a coherent background.

But what sort of things should I know about my world beyond my story and my characters?

That's where this book comes in.

In the following chapters, you'll find questions and exercises designed to help you iron out the details of your world. Some of them are obvious: what are the different cultures in your world? Do they get along? Who is in charge?

Some of them are not-so-obvious: what are the historical interactions that led to the current relationships? Why did things work out the way they did? How much history do your characters know?

A comedian once explained how he would never cheat on his wife because he had worked out the possible scenarios in his mind beforehand and decided how he would behave if the situation should present itself.[1] Consider this book your chance to have all sorts of conversations with your characters so that when they are in a situation, you won't have to stop to work out the world mechanics—you will already know! Many of the answers you create will not explicitly feature in your story but knowing them in the back of your mind will make the story you write more believable.

---

[1] The joke, of course, was that he had never had that conversation with himself about robbing a train (Bert Kreischer: The Machine!).

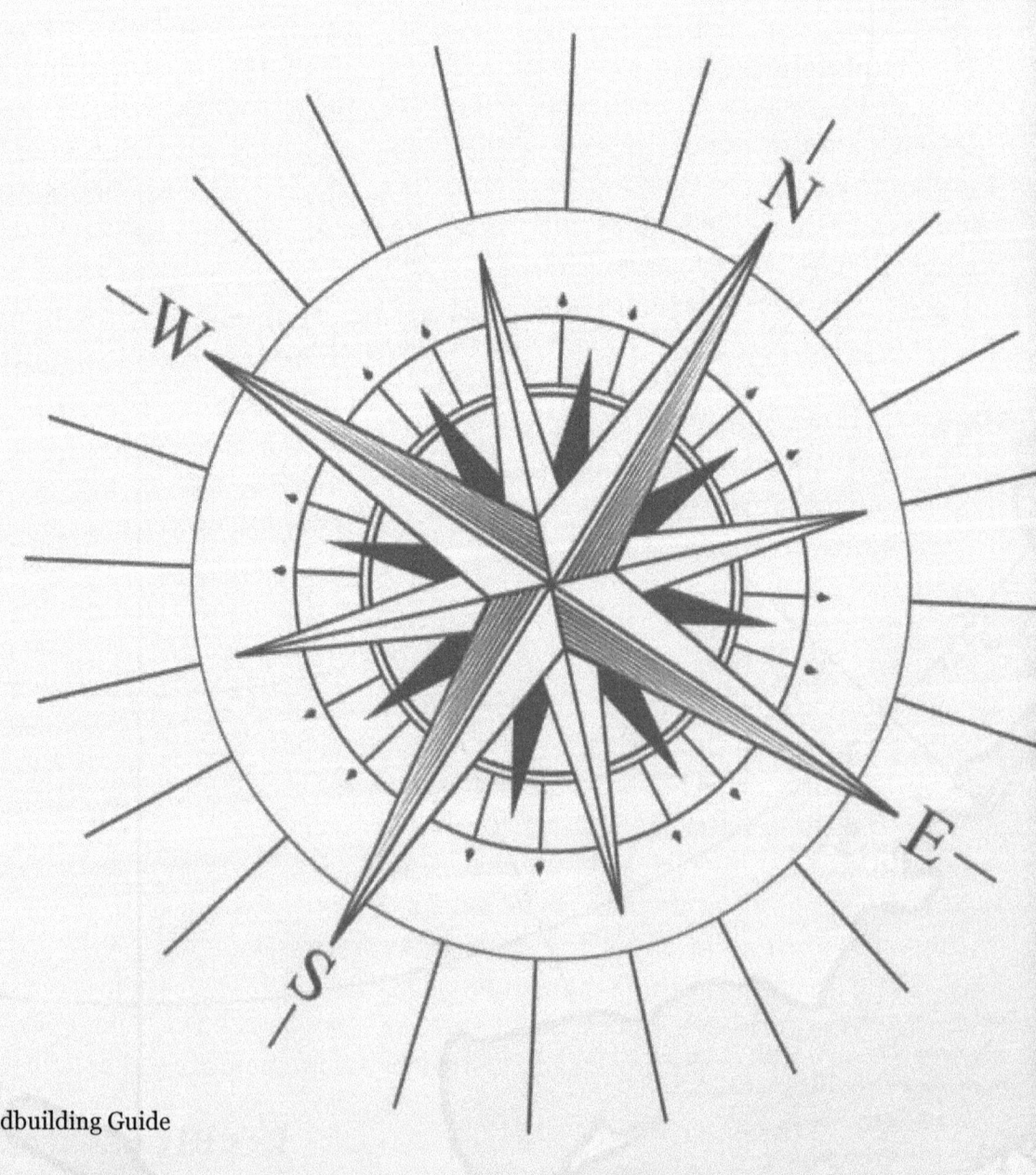

Why You Should Trust Me

I've been writing for a long time (so says every writer, right?). I've published novels, short stories, textbooks, and monographs. I even published my dissertation and nothing in life takes planning like writing a dissertation. If you have not done one, you may never know the level of rabbit hole research you can get into. Sticky notes used to cover my walls when I was hip-deep in that odyssey.

I've learned a much cleaner organization system since then—and I'm still learning every day. I teach composition classes to college students—and I learn from them as well, rediscovering my love for writing in both their pointed questions and their rambling discussions. I'm always eager to learn a new way of doing something, especially if it will save me time.

Honestly, my characters run circles around me. I'm not trustworthy—that's why I need this book! I often find myself pausing in the middle of a scene to dive into the history or mechanics of my world, knowing I should have figured them out beforehand. When I wrote my Klauden's Ring series, I had to re-read entire books to make sure I didn't screw up the details before I began writing the next book.

That said, I've developed tried and true questions I now ask myself (fifteen novels into my writing career) when I get a new idea for a story. They help me flesh out as much of the world and backstory as I can before I jump into the writing, so I don't have to lose momentum addressing these details in the moment. That's the honest answer, but now for the rest of it.

After creating this Worldbuilding Book, I wondered how much time I would have saved if I had this book handy.

The answer is hour and hours, so now I take the time, do the exercises, and get my background settled. I still don't use all of them, but that's the idea of the book. Answer what is helpful to you and your story and ignore the rest.

I hope you find this book useful in developing and recording your world—even if that means the exercises prompt deeper thoughts about the details. I know I'll be using this book to help me stay organized as I write my dragon shifter series!

What is Worldbuilding?

Worldbuilding is what creative writers do when they form the framework that contains their story. It includes everything from the layout of the furniture in someone's bedroom and the geography of the city they live in, to the languages spoken by their fellow inhabitants and the technological capabilities of the society that surrounds them. It's the details that bring a story to life—the thing that separates a decent tale from a life-changing epic adventure that every single one of the reader's friends must read immediately. It gives a story depth and richness and the sense that there is more beyond the page, that readers could find a pulsing, vibrant existence beyond the edges of the pages they are reading.

How can you provide this magical transformative experience for your readers? Do your homework. Build your world before you step into it (or before you finish stepping out of it on that last page!) so readers feel the world lives beyond the moments they see in the story.

Here's a quick list to keep in mind when making your way through this book:

1. There is not a predetermined order to building your world (unless you want it that way!). You can flip from building the map to deciding the fashion to creating the calendar, then flop to debating how medicine works and hopping back to wars in your world. Record the details as they come to you.

2. This may seem like homework for you as a writer, but you are not obligated to answer every question. Think of it as documenting the way you weave the story you are creating. Focus on the sections that make sense for your story and your world. There are a lot of questions but don't let that overwhelm you. Again, this should be a fun part of the creative process. Feel free to skip around.

3. Have some fun with the activities spread throughout each section, but don't wrack your brain to finish them all down to the last detail. You will not be graded.

4. I know you're excited that you know every single ruler for the last five hundred years of a dynasty, but do your readers need to know all of that right now? Probably not. Sometimes this is called the iceberg effect: you are aware of everything under the water, but the story you are telling might just be the tip. When you add these details to your story, be sure to slide them in as a natural addition to the scene rather than as an info-dump. A good rule of thumb is to hint at it, be confident that you know the names (maybe have a mnemonic song to get the order right like the British have for their monarchs over the years) but let that background info seep into the story in the right place and the right time.

5. Writing is work and can be hard at times, but it should also be fun. If you'd rather be writing the story itself, then close this book and do that instead! Just remember the questions are here when you're ready to build more of the scaffolding that will hold your story up. Keep it next to you and pop information into it as your story is flowing.

6. YOU GOT THIS!

How to Use This Book

This book is divided into six sections. The first five focus on creating your world, and the last section contains resources for recording specific details.

- Part One: Big Picture issues like creation, gods, myths, legends, and heroes (and villains).

- Part Two: Cultural issues beginning with maps, then addressing government, society, cultural practices, warfare, and appearance.

- Part Three: Underlying social issues involving economy, education, relationships, communication, technology, travel, and health and wellness.

- Part Four: Mechanics of the world with questions about science, nature, weather, and measurements (time and distance).

- Part Five: People and creatures that live in your world.

- Part Six: Resources such as character cards, plot points, general notes, and "top fives."

Each section begins with general open-ended questions designed to promote critical thinking about the topic. After you've considered the broader picture, you're ready to drill down to specific questions. Each section ends with the same idea: how much does the average person in your world know about that topic? Then, there are a few questions that ask you to distinguish your world from the world we live in, the Primary World known as Earth. (How is your fictional world similar to the one readers inhabit? How is it different?) After that, each section concludes with creative activities to generate content that may come in handy while writing. (Need a random song that's being sung in the background of your bar scene? Done!)

As the creator of this book, the topics are arranged in a way that makes sense for my brain, but that doesn't mean it will work for your process. Skip around as needed. Use the section that appeals to you at the moment. I promise, the only test is the one your readers will give you when they start asking pointed questions about the background details!

Part One: In the beginning

This section deals with the Big Picture or how your world came to be. The Creation section asks questions about the beginning of your entire world while the Gods section focuses on supernatural beings. From there, this section drills down to Myths and Legends and ends with Heroes.

A. Creation

1. How did your world come into being? Was it formed out of the Void, the result of some cosmic boom, or the plaything of a godlike being? Tolkien's Middle Earth began as a song of the Ainur, a vision in music that the Valar had to build based on their understanding and memories of the experience.

_____

_____

_____

2. Is there one world/planet? Is it a free-floating ball in space or a disc with an edge that people can fall off? Terry Pratchett's Discworld is literally a disc on top of four elephants on top of a turtle that swims through space.

_____

_____

_____

3. Is the world part of a larger galaxy/universe? Is there a larger cosmos with other solar systems in the galaxy or just the lone world floating in the void by itself? Think about the night sky your inhabitants would see—are the lights in the sky stars or something else (Shrek's ogre ancestors, for instance)?

_____

_____

_____

4. How big is the universe? Are other worlds nearby or far away? Can people see neighboring planets or travel to them? How is this done? The answer will connect with your technology section, but for now, get a general sense. For example, the sun is 91.4 million miles from Earth while the moon is only 238,900 miles away. If the speed of light is 186,282.397 miles per second, how far away is your world from everything else?

___

5. Is there a multiverse, or more than one world stacked atop one another, perhaps connected by portals or wormholes? Bonus question—if the answer is yes, are there multiple versions of your characters? Multiple timelines with different outcomes? How does this affect your story? Rick and Morty want to know!

___

6. How do those worlds, if they exist, relate to each other? Do the events in World A affect World B, like a bomb in one world creating a deadland in another (Think Stephen King's *Wastelands* in the Dark Tower series)? Does a person exist simultaneously in all worlds at once?

___

7. For the people in your world, are there visible stars in the sky? Other planets that can be seen? Do people create constellations from the patterns? What meaning is attributed to these lights in the sky? Is astrology a thing in your world?

_____
_____
_____

8. How big is the world? How long would it take someone to travel around it? Eighty days in a weather balloon or a year on foot? (See Section 3F for more questions on Travel.)

_____
_____
_____

9. How is the land on the world laid out? Are there multiple continents? How possible is it to travel from one to the other? What lies between these chunks of land? Are there monsters in the deep ocean or unknown dangers in the wide gaps between civilizations?

_____
_____
_____

10. Has anyone seen the planet from beyond the surface? Do people travel to space to get perspective? Do they think the world is flat or ends beyond the mountain range in the distance?

_____
_____
_____

11. What is the climate of each continent? Is part of it desert or swamp or windswept plains? Where are the mountain ranges? Can people cross them to explore other areas? Think about Tolkien's Gap of Rohan or the Mines of Moria (even Caradhras) as the only nearby paths across the Misty Mountains (and how that geography affects the storyline). (See Section 2A for more questions on Maps.)

_____

_____

12. What about water in the world? Are there oceans/seas? How big are they? How deep are they? Are there lost civilizations beneath the waves? How comfortable are the people traveling over water? Is access to boats a problem for some people?

_____

_____

13. Is the ocean/sea potable or salt? Is fresh water hard to come by? Can certain people drink salt water in your world? (See Section 4A for more questions on Science.)

_____

_____

14. What is the weather like? How are the seasons organized? Is it standard four seasons with cold weather to the north or something else? Many fantasy worlds have created calendars complete with seasonal names, months, and days of the week. (See Section 4D for more questions on Time.)

_____

_____

Part One: In the beginning

15. Has the world always looked like the present day or has it changed over time? Was there an age of dinosaurs and prehistoric plant life? Was your world covered in oceans, or has it always been as it is now? (This relates to the "how old is your world" question, too!).

___
___
___

16. If the topography has changed, what happened to make it look different? Was this change a result of a natural catastrophe (meteor strike, volcano eruption, ice age, etc.) or the result of the people who live in the world? What did the people do that caused such dramatic shifts in the world? Even earth has had dramatic environmental shifts over time (*cough* dinosaurs *cough*).

___
___
___

17. How old is the world? Does the world have an expiration date—like will the sun explode at some point or the gravitational pull let it drift away into the void—or will the world always be there?

___
___
___

11. What is the climate of each continent? Is part of it desert or swamp or windswept plains? Where are the mountain ranges? Can people cross them to explore other areas? Think about Tolkien's Gap of Rohan or the Mines of Moria (even Caradhras) as the only nearby paths across the Misty Mountains (and how that geography affects the storyline). (See Section 2A for more questions on Maps.)

_____

_____

12. What about water in the world? Are there oceans/seas? How big are they? How deep are they? Are there lost civilizations beneath the waves? How comfortable are the people traveling over water? Is access to boats a problem for some people?

_____

_____

13. Is the ocean/sea potable or salt? Is fresh water hard to come by? Can certain people drink salt water in your world? (See Section 4A for more questions on Science.)

_____

_____

14. What is the weather like? How are the seasons organized? Is it standard four seasons with cold weather to the north or something else? Many fantasy worlds have created calendars complete with seasonal names, months, and days of the week. (See Section 4D for more questions on Time.)

_____

_____

Part One: In the beginning

15. Has the world always looked like the present day or has it changed over time? Was there an age of dinosaurs and prehistoric plant life? Was your world covered in oceans, or has it always been as it is now? (This relates to the "how old is your world" question, too!).

___

16. If the topography has changed, what happened to make it look different? Was this change a result of a natural catastrophe (meteor strike, volcano eruption, ice age, etc.) or the result of the people who live in the world? What did the people do that caused such dramatic shifts in the world? Even earth has had dramatic environmental shifts over time (*cough* dinosaurs *cough*).

___

17. How old is the world? Does the world have an expiration date—like will the sun explode at some point or the gravitational pull let it drift away into the void—or will the world always be there?

___

18. Are there immortals who remember the beginning? How accurate is that recollection (and do they share that knowledge with others)? Often the writers of histories have a specific perspective that will shape the story they record—how have these immortals framed the history they recall? Will those beings be around for the end of the world like the robots in *AI*?

_____

_____

_____

_____

_____

19. How much does the average person know about the creation of the world? Is this knowledge protected or is it shared? How do people share this information (*Giver*-style or oral culture or what)?

_____

_____

_____

_____

_____

A1. Earth-Variant Creation

1. If your world is loosely based on the real world, how is it different from the known universe?

   _____
   _____
   _____

2. What world-features are your characters familiar with that readers will recognize?

   _____
   _____
   _____

3. What distinct world-features have you added to distinguish your world from the real one?

   _____
   _____
   _____

4. Do things in the universe have the same name the scientific community uses (Big Bang, quarks, Jupiter, Io, etc.)?

___

5. Is Pluto a planet or a planetoid in your world?

Part One: In the beginning   9

1. Creation Fun Activity: Mapmaking

Maps can be generated in so many ways (online, hand-drawn, stolen from real places, etc.), but this is a fun method if you want an element of chance.

YOU WILL NEED:

- a blank piece of paper or tabletop (even better if your tabletop can be written on with Dry-Erase markers!). This space should be bigger than your map will be; trust me, you need the space.
- markers (Dry-Erase, if possible) or preferred writing utensils
- a handful of multi-sided dice (d4s, d6s, d8s, d10s, d12s, and d20s)
    - You can find dice at any gaming shop, comic book store, or online retailer.

SETUP FIRST: decide what your dice stand for. Below is a possible way to do this but feel free to play with these categories.

D4s—Settlement:
1-crossroads
2-village
3-town
4-city

D6s—Land Type:
1-desert
2-forest
3-plains
4-mountains
5-swamp
6-jungle

D8s—Water Feature:
1-stream
2-river
3-lake
4-ocean
5-waterfall
6-rapids
7-dam
8-pond

D10s—Roads:
1-dirt path
2-cobblestone track
3-forest path
4-wagon road
5-trade route
6-secret road
7-mountain pass
8-secret passage
9-cliffside path
10-uncrossable barrier

D12s—Features:

1-small farm
2-secret underground cave
3-uninhabitable bogland
2-bridge over something
3-ancient ruin
4-government seat
5-old battleground
6-dormant volcano
7-active volcano
8-glacier
9-hot springs
10-large farming community
11-prospering kingdom
12-abandoned kingdom

D20s—Random Bits:

1-sunken treasure
2-cursed tomb
3-huge monster lair
4-nuisance creature home
5-haunted forest
6-mass graveyard
7-religious retreat
8-secret underground city
9-hero/heroine's home
10-bird's eyrie
11-historical landmark
12-undiscovered country
13-impassable lands
14-dangerous territory
15-unpredictable ground
16-sanctuary
17-poisonous plants
18-super rare plants
19-contested territory
20-here there be dragons!

Now you're ready to let fate decide what your world looks like! Throw the dice and mark down the meaning of each number. Some numbers won't work—why is there an ocean inside my forest?—but you can play around until your world comes into focus!

NOT EVERYONE CAN FREEHAND MAPS—SO USE SOFTWARE TO CREATE ONE INSTEAD. WONDERDRAFT IS PRETTY COOL...

Legend:
- Mountains
- Water
- Desert
- Wall
- Forrest
- Bridge
- Housing

2. Alternate Creation Fun Activity

Sketch your world map in the space below!

12 The General Worldbuilding Guide

2a.
Super-Secret Alternate Fun Activity

Or use an existing map and build your world there!

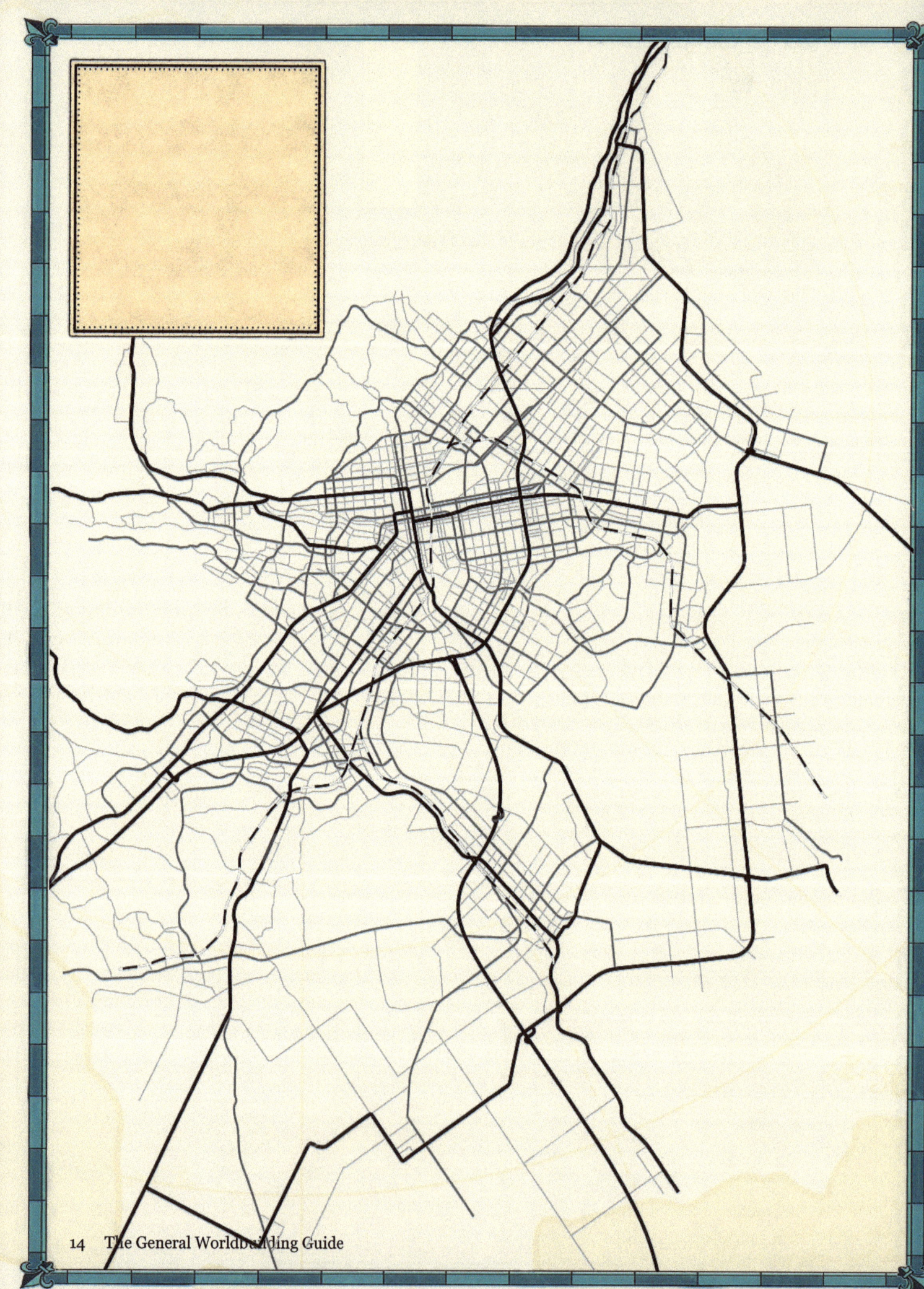

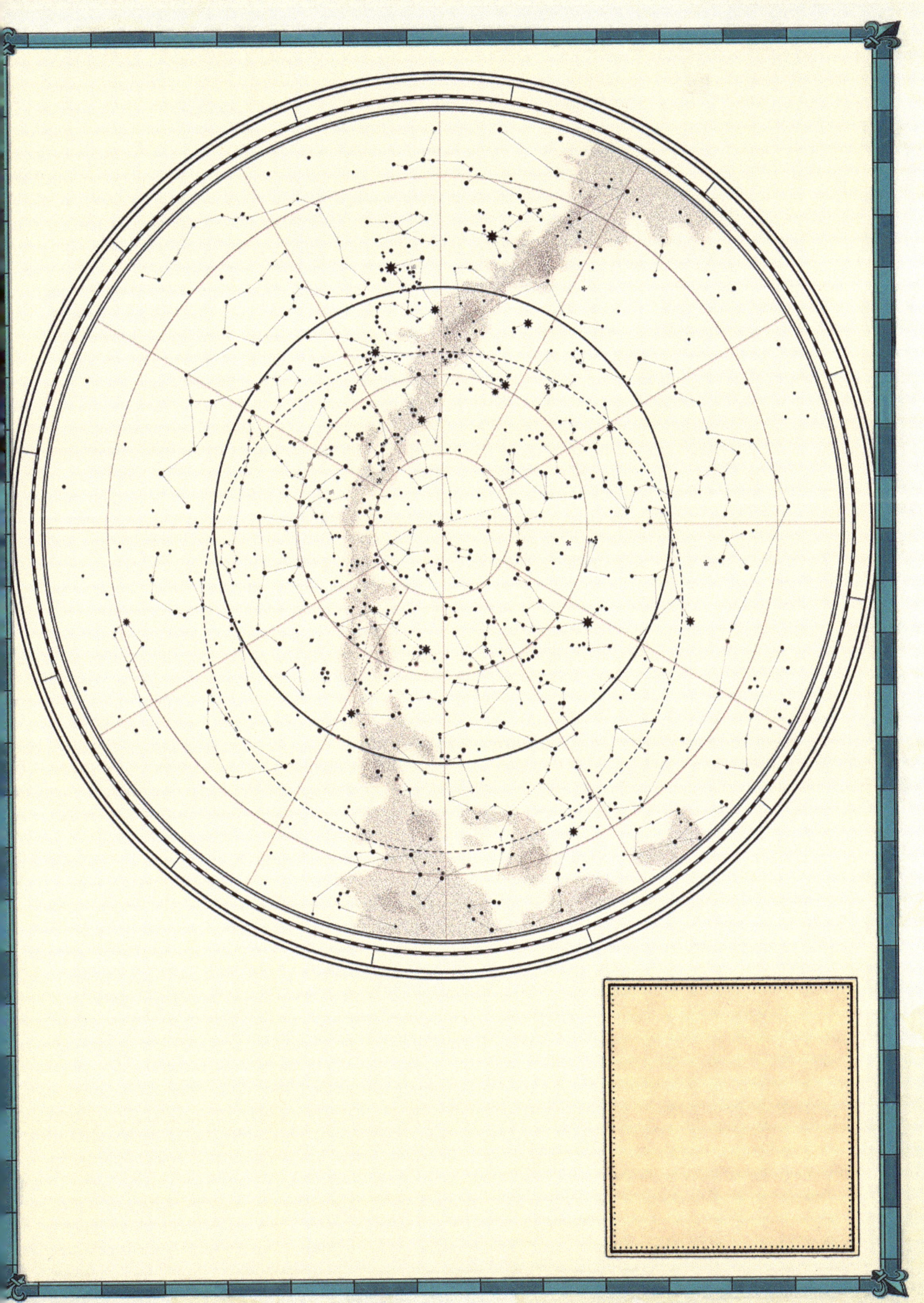

B. Gods

1. Are there gods in your world? If so, it's time to start a chart (see page 25)! Who controls what domain and why?

   _____
   _____
   _____

2. Did the gods create the world or was it Big Bang–style? Did the Titans create the world or will Fenrir the Wolf swallow the sun?

   _____
   _____
   _____

3. What are the gods called (Ainur, Powers, Witches)? Do they have different names in different cultures?

   _____
   _____
   _____

4. Who worships which ones? Has this caused conflict over time? (See Section 2E for more question on Warfare.)

_____
_____
_____

5. Are the gods real? How debated is this in your world? Do your characters know the answer?

_____
_____
_____

6. Did the inhabitants of the world create stories about gods based on nature myths (Thor is really thunder, etc.)?

_____
_____
_____

7. Do the gods interact with the beings in the world? How? Do they speak directly to the inhabitants or speak through a medium (oracles, prophecies, bird signs, etc.)?

_____
_____
_____
_____

Part One: In the beginning 17

8. If they do, how do other people view those who are god-touched? Is this a gift or a curse? How do the other gods view those who "meddle" with the people in the world?

_____
_____
_____
_____
_____

9. Did they previously interact but haven't in a long time? Why? What happened to stop them? Are the gods asleep like in *Erik the Viking*?

_____
_____
_____

10. Do the gods breed with inhabitants, creating demigods? Do half-gods go to camp like Percy Jackson? Is this a known practice or something secret? Do mortal children inherit god-like powers?

_____
_____
_____

11. What would those creatures look like? Create a handful of possible demigods so you have an idea of what this path could look like.

_____
_____
_____

The General Worldbuilding Guide

12. What makes a god? Can an ordinary person become a god, or do you have to be born as one? What powers do the gods possess?

_____
_____
_____

13. Are godly powers fixed or can they steal them/swap them/lose them/fight over them? Are the powers inherent or bestowed by a magic item (which can be stolen, swapped, lost, etc.)?

_____
_____
_____

14. What motivates the gods in your world? What do they want? Do they let the others in the world know their desires? How do they let their will be known—burning bush, dreams, ominous visions?

_____
_____
_____

15. How does the divine motivation compare to what your characters want? Is this a cause of conflict in your story (man vs god)?

_____
_____
_____

16. How much power do the gods have? Is there a limit? Who determines the limit and how? Can gods kill/resurrect people? Can they control people's bodies/decisions/thoughts?

___

17. Do the people in your world have free will? Can your characters change their fate? In the Cedric series by Valerie Willis, characters are constantly interacting with the gods and altering their destinies.

___

18. How much of the future is known by the gods? Can they predict the actions of others? Do they control the destiny of the inhabitants of your world? Is destiny foretold or is it just random happenstance?

___

19. Are there prophecies in your world? How much importance do the inhabitants place on these words? This is often a catalyst in many stories—*Harry Potter*, *Star Wars*, *Lord of the Rings*, every fantasy novel, etc.

___

20. Who delivers the prophecies of the gods? Is there a special class of inhabitants for this purpose? Describe the process. (Drink this drugged elixir, then have visions and convulsions while telling scribes what is seen?)

_____
_____
_____

21. Do people believe the prophecies? Why or why not? Maybe only certain people—if so, who? Do your main characters believe them?

_____
_____
_____

22. Why do certain people believe in these things? Is there a benefit to belief? (*Pascal's Wager*-style or something else?)

_____
_____
_____

23. Is there organized religion in the world? What does it look like? How does it affect your characters?

_____
_____
_____

Part One: In the beginning

24. Is there more than one religion? How do followers of each religion feel about the others? (This is a great time for another chart!)

___

25. How much does the average person know about the world of the gods?

B1: Earth-Variant Gods

1. Do your gods fall into a specific pantheon that readers will recognize? In what ways are your gods canon and how have you shifted them?

_____
_____
_____

2. How much influence will traditional stories about those gods have on their actions in your story?

_____
_____
_____

3. How familiar do readers need to be with this pantheon in order to pick up on hints or foreshadowing? Should you give backstory, just in case your readers don't know who Apollo or Ra or Odin are?

_____
_____
_____

4. What classic works about this pantheon have you used for reference? For Greek mythology, are you using Homer or moving into Ovid? What sources are you relying on, and how do they compare to other source material about these gods?

_____

_____

_____

5. What drew you to this pantheon in the first place? Why use these gods and not your own creations?

_____

_____

_____

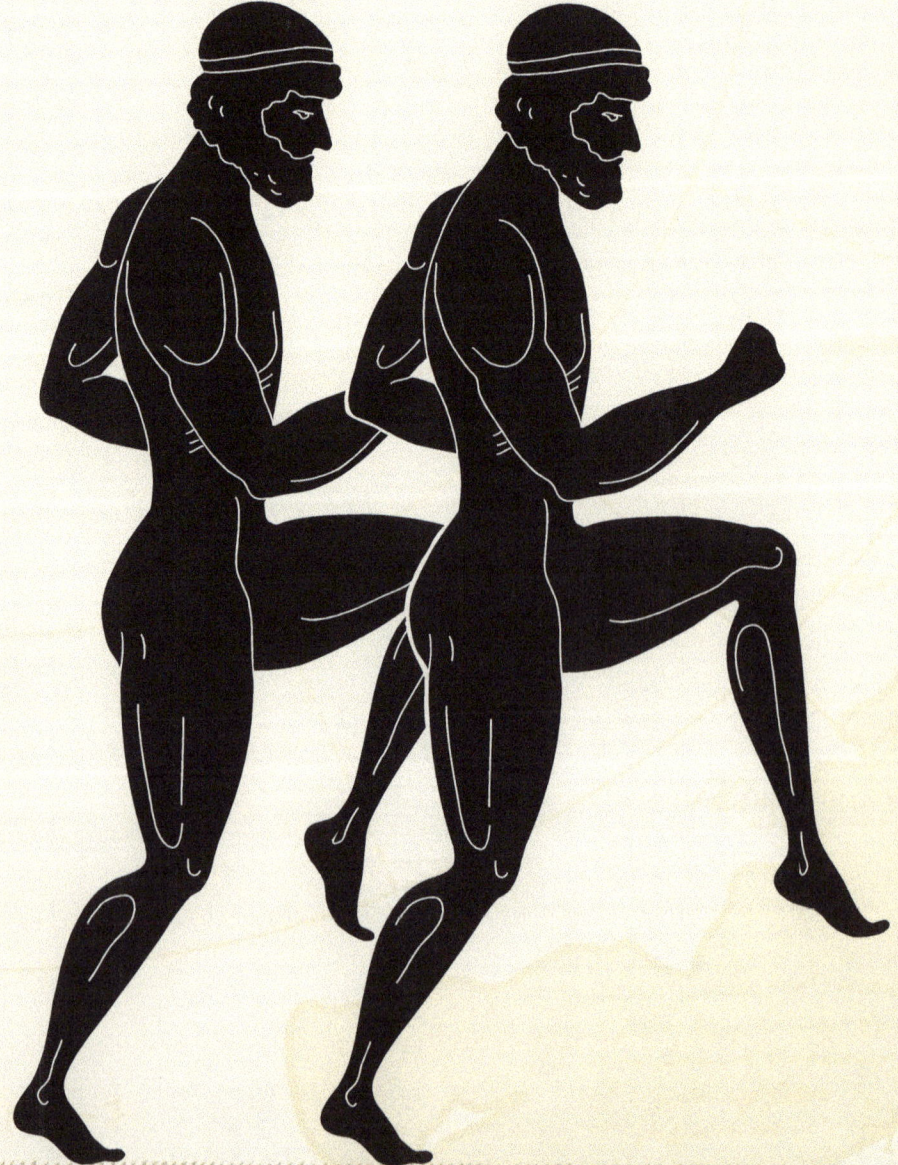

3. Gods Fun Activity: Pick Your Powers

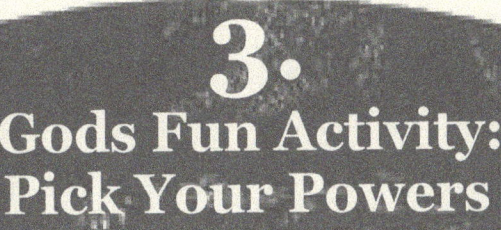

It's time to lay out the theology for your world!
Who are the players in your world?

Name	Hera				
Domain/area of control	Marriage/ Domesticity/ family/childbirth				
Powers	Strength, immortality, bless/ curse mortals, eternal youth, mind control				
Backstory	Sister-Wife of Zeus, Mother of Hebe and Hephaestus (Area, Eris, etc.)				
likes	Athena (sometimes)				
dislikes	Trojans, Aphrodite, Zeus's other women, Heracles				
Major supportive city	Argos, Mycenae				
Associated symbols/signs	Cows, cuckoos, ducks				
Other names	Juno				
Interactions with characters					

4. Character Building Activity: Connect the Dots

Now that you have some gods in mind, think about how these forces interact with your characters in this story.

- What is the goal of the gods?

  _____
  _____
  _____
  _____

- What motivates them to behave as they do in relation to your characters?

  _____
  _____
  _____
  _____

- What is the central conflict your characters will face in terms of divine intervention?

  _____
  _____
  _____
  _____

Now let's flip the script back to your characters:

- What is the goal of your characters in relation to the gods?

  _____
  _____
  _____
  _____
  _____
  _____

- What motivates your characters in relation to the gods? Does your hero have a connection with a specific deity that pushes them to action?

  _____
  _____
  _____
  _____
  _____
  _____

- What is the central conflict that your characters must face in terms of divine interference?

  _____
  _____
  _____
  _____
  _____
  _____

C. Myths and Legends

1. What stories do inhabitants have about the early days of the world? Are these passed down orally or written in a sacred book or just shared with everyone all the time?

___

2. Are these myths true? If true, how accurate are the renditions the inhabitants share currently? Have things been exaggerated? (More miracles! Bigger fish!)

___

3. If the myths are not true, where did they come from? Who created them and why? (Is there a Bene Gesserit or Aes Sedai group tasked with managing these stories?)

___

4. Are there myths about natural phenomena? Lightning/seasons/etc.? Do people believe these stories, or are they told to children to keep them from being scared (or to scare them away from dangerous things: "Don't go into the woods. Wolves eat lost children.")?

___
___
___
___

5. Are these myths/explanations universal or specific to people/region? Are there major differences or just minor alterations between versions? Sketch out a rough version of popular myths that most people in your world would know (America: Mickey Mouse, Disney Princesses, *Star Wars*, *Harry Potter*, etc.).

___
___
___
___

6. Are there legends about exceptional people? Who are the heroes in this world, and are they different from the gods, if there are gods? Do they have stories of Zeus and Shiva but also of Achilles and Io? What about Cuchulainn or Mannan Mac Lir? Andraste? Merlin? What do people consider heroic and worthy of storytelling? (The next section expands on this!)

___
___
___
___

Part One: In the beginning 29

7. What value do the people place on these stories—educational, cautionary tale, moral lesson? Should Hamlet be emulated or avoided?

___

8. Do people argue about myths and legends? Is this just something to talk about after dinner to pass the time or a topic people feel is important enough to fight over?

___

9. How do current inhabitants know these stories? Word of mouth? Books? Annual celebrations? Traveling performer reenactments? Communal memories?

___

10. How much does the average person know about myths and legends in your world?

___

C1:
Earth-Variant Myths and Legends

1. Do your myths and legends fall into a specific pantheon that readers may recognize? How have you adjusted these stories to fit your purpose in this story? Danielle Orsino's Birth of the Fae series takes traditional stories of angels and twists them into fae instead.

   _____
   _____
   _____

2. How much do you expect readers to recognize in these stories? Do they need to be familiar with specific events in the stories in order to recognize foreshadowing/important hints/etc.? Mark Tarrant plays with the Peter Pan story in *The Mighty Hook*, but his version of the story may surprise some readers (Hint: Peter Pan isn't the hero.)

   _____
   _____
   _____

3. Poll time: ask your friends if they are familiar with the stories you are using—not the friends who already geek out about it with you—your other friends who are into other things. Has the story reached popular culture in the way you think? (I always assume everyone knows about *Star Wars*—newsflash: they don't!)

   _____
   _____
   _____

4. Why did you choose these stories to embed in your world? What is the significance—to you? To your characters?

___

5. How will these stories affect the story you are telling? What part do myths and legends play in your own life? How does that compare to the way you treat them in your story?

___

5. Myths and Legends Fun Activity: Create Legends, Myths, and Folk Tales!

A **LEGEND** is a story, usually about a person, that has some basis in factual events but may have grown in the telling. The truth or facts are still dominant in the story, though the meaning is also relevant. A popular legend would be Robin Hood, whose popular story is very different from the historical record! (Check out Wynken de Worde for the earliest facts.)

A **MYTH** is a story that explains a natural phenomenon or has a significant cultural meaning to specific people. The story often has to do with the origin of a people and may have sacred or religious overtones. The facts are less important than the overall meaning in a myth. Some common myths would be the Iroquois turtle for the world or Persephone and Hades for the seasons.

And while we're here, let's cover **FOLK TALES**, often including fairy tales and fables. Folk tales are stories passed down orally by common people (folk) that impart a moral lesson. Fairy tales often involve an ordinary person's adventures in the land of Faerie. (See Tolkien's "On Fairy Stories" for a detailed discussion!) Fables also teach a moral lesson but feature animals instead of humans.

Take a moment and sketch out three stories that your characters would know. No need to write novels here—just a general idea: slow turtle, fast rabbit, *slow and steady wins the race*; or cursed princess asleep in tower, handsome prince, magic kiss, *happily ever after*. You can use the chart below to get started!

This is a modified version of Freytag's model of fiction. *Exposition* refers to any background information readers learn at the start. *Rising action* builds the story up and *falling action* brings it to a close, but fiction also includes a *conflict* made up of the *climax*, the most important moment in the plot, and the *crisis*, the most important emotional point in the story. Stories end with a *resolution*, and by the end, readers should grasp some basic lesson.

Part One: In the beginning

Obviously, not all stories follow this format (the fun ones break all the rules, right?). For this exercise the goal is to have a short tale ready for reference. You can write that book when you finish this one! (Think Rowling's *Tales of Beedle the Bard*.)

Names	Hansel and Gretel			
Exposition	Evil mom/stepmother, weak father; lost or abandoned children in the woods			
Rising Action	Pebble trail; breadcrumb trail; candy cottage in the woods			
Conflict: Climax and Crisis	Outwitting the witch; killing the witch; saving each other			
Falling Action	Getting out of the house alive			
Resolution	Grateful to be alive; get treasure			
Lesson	Family matters; don't trust witches; gluttony			

The General Worldbuilding Guide

- What kind of stories are popular in your world? Do people like fairy tales and happy endings, or do they prefer horror stories with awful endings?

  _____
  _____
  _____
  _____
  _____

- Do your characters like what everyone else likes, or are they different somehow?

  _____
  _____
  _____
  _____
  _____
  _____

D. I Need a Hero

1. Who are the heroes in this world? Whom do inhabitants look up to? Can ordinary people be heroes, or are there special requirements?

   _____
   _____
   _____

2. How true/accurate are the versions of the heroic tales inhabitants currently know? Are these exaggerated versions of what happened? Did any of them happen at all (or did Jasker make the Witcher a hero)?

   _____
   _____
   _____

3. What do inhabitants use these stories for—instruct children/warn youth? Are these tales to emulate, or are they cautionary tales to scare people? Do people want to like their heroes, or should they learn from their mistakes?

   _____
   _____
   _____

4. Do certain areas (towns, countries) have specific national heroes? Who are they? How much do other cultures know about those heroes? Are one culture's heroes another culture's villains?

_____
_____
_____
_____

5. What does the average person expect when someone uses the word "hero"? Do they imagine a person running into a burning building or frontline healthcare worker treating patients with deadly communicable diseases or the single parent who gets out of bed to face the day? Is a supernatural being helping those who don't share their powers?

_____
_____
_____
_____

6. Are certain qualities prized by certain inhabitants? What are those features? Why are those the traits people seek in heroes? Do your heroes have to be physically pleasing or have inner beauty? (Quasimodo or Esmerelda?)

_____
_____
_____
_____

Part One: In the beginning 37

7. Do your heroes uphold the status quo or fight to remake the world? Do heroes in this world fight for or against opposing powers? Why? (Just think about *The Boys*.)

_____
_____
_____

8. Are people considered heroes while still alive, or does the person need to be dead in order to achieve worship? Do people only enjoy stories of a hero after the event, or do your characters appreciate the hero while it's happening?

_____
_____
_____

9. How does the average person feel about the popular heroes of the day?

_____
_____
_____

10. Is heroism a result of action or birthright in your world? Are you born a hero or made into one? Colossus says there are only a few moments that make a hero—is this how it works?

11. Is there a recurring story about heroes that resonates with all of the inhabitants of the world, regardless of race or location (like Joseph Campbell's hero myth)?

12. How are heroes used in the world? Do those in power use these stories for a specific purpose (to oppress certain people, to uphold other people/cultures)? Are certain stories encouraged while others are outlawed?

13. Are there anti-heroes in your world? What qualities do they possess? Do people root for the underdog, the bad guy, the hero's adversary? Is the line between hero and villain very clear to your characters, or does it blur at times?

Part One: In the beginning 39

14. How much does the average person know about heroes in your world?

_____

_____

_____

D1: Earth-Variant Heroes

1. How do your heroes compare to the stories we have in our world? Do you have your own version of the runs-into-burning-building, lifts-car-off-child, saves-world-from-supervillain, sacrifices-self-for-greater-good trope?

___

2. How have you shifted/altered your heroes for your story? Why did you make these changes?

___

3. Poll time: think about your character's heroes. Who do they look up to and why? How do these heroes compare to those of your friends and family in this world?

___

4. Heroes are something that vary from person to person—what do you value in a hero? What qualities matter to you? Why those and not something else?

_____
_____
_____

5. Think about the heroes you have admired in your life. Has this list changed over time? Why? Do you think your characters' preferences may shift over the course of the story as well?

_____
_____
_____

6. Heroic Fun Activity: Heroes and Villains

Use the chart below to make a brief list of the **HEROES** and **VILLAINS** in your world that your characters would know about.

- Who are these people and what do your characters know about them?
- What qualities do they possess that make them worthy of worship or disdain?

	Hero	Hero	Villain	Villain
Name				
Story				
Summary of story				
Qualities that make them heroic/villainous				
Qualities your characters admire (yes, even for villains!)				
Qualities your characters dislike (yes, even for heroes!)				

Part One: In the beginning

7. Character Building Activity: Name Your Characters' Heroes!

Think about who your characters would idolize in our world. Instead of the heroes covered in the previous activity, choose heroes from our world (Thor, Athena, Captain America, Rosie the Riveter, your mom, etc.). Why would your characters look up to them (if they knew who they were)?

Character	Klauden van Sherinak			
Hero(es)	Carl Sagan			
Reasons	Klauden would appreciate Sagan's constant quest for answers and his need to understand the world around him.			

The General Worldbuilding Guide

Build Your World Activities

Now that you've considered how your world came into being, what kinds of divine intervention are likely, and what stories the inhabitants tell about it, it's time to think about how these details relate to your story specifically.

8. Opposites Attract: What is the tension in your world?

Often, we describe things by contrasting them with unlike things. It is "this" because it is not "that." Categorizing concepts is easier when we place them in opposition to other concepts. Take a moment to consider how tension works in your world.

ELEMENTS—In our world, water is the opposite of fire.

- How do elements interact in your world? What forces are in opposition?
- How does the tension between these elements affect your story?

GODS—No matter the mythology, you will find gods at odds with one another whether based on personality, history, or on domain/region of control.

- How do these forces work in your world? Which powers oppose one another? Melkor vs Manwe? Hera vs Athena? Thor vs Loki?
- How do these interactions affect your story?

ENVIRONMENTS—In our world, we often think of places as they contrast with other places. A desert is dry compared to a rainforest. A sunny beach contrasts with Montana in January. "Oh, we don't go to the Bad Place anymore."

- How do the people of your world think about environments? Are there certain places that are the default contrast to others?
- Where can you use these descriptions in your story?

What are other key contrasts that are important to your story? Make a chart, jot down a list, or take notes on how these things relate to one another.

9. Build a Timeline for your World

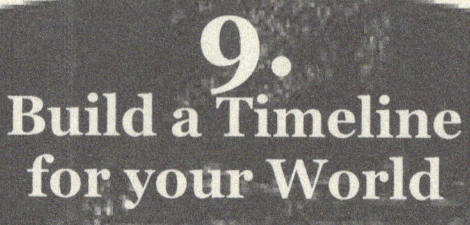

ANNALS are an ancient method of tracking major events in the world in a short set of observations. Think about the history of your world in the broadest strokes.

- How old is your world?
- What are the major world events (that matter for your story)?
- How are those events related to one another? (This famine led to that civil war which caused these people to invade and led to the death of your hero's mother in battle.)

Date	Event	Effect on Story (Why should readers care about this?)

Date	Event	Effect on Story (Why should readers care about this?)

Build Your World Activities

Date	Event	Effect on Story (Why should readers care about this?)

10. Your Story Time: In the Beginning

Now it's time to take notes on how this *information* will affect the story you have in mind. It's okay if the answer to some of these questions is "**ABSOLUTELY NOTHING AT ALL!**" Even if this information doesn't come into play directly, it's good to have it in the back of your mind in case an eager reader writes an email asking about it one day—you'll have a ready reply!

1. You've created a planet/solar system/galaxy/universe. How does this creation method affect your story?

   _____
   _____
   _____

2. You've created some gods and thought about how they interact with your world. How will these parameters affect your story?

   _____
   _____
   _____

3. You've thought about myths and legends that are popular in your world. How will these tales come up in your story? Will your characters talk about those stories (or even about themselves as characters in a story like Frodo and Sam)?

   _____
   _____
   _____

Build Your World Activities

4. You've considered what makes a hero in your world. How will these heroic characteristics (or the heroes themselves) come into play in your story?

_____
_____
_____

5. You've thought about tension in your world. How will these oppositional forces affect your story?

_____
_____
_____

6. You've worked out a timeline for your world. How will these events affect your story, specifically?

_____
_____
_____

Use this space to jot down any other ideas that this exercise may have sparked—they will be useful at some point!

Part Two:
The world is ... complicated

This section deals with the nitty gritty details of the world. It starts with bigger issues like Maps, Government, Society, Cultural Practices, then drills down into Warfare and Appearance.

A. Maps and the Known World

1. Do you have a map of your world? If it's a fantasy novel, you should! You can draw your own or use computer software to help you out!

　
　
　

2. Does the average inhabitant have access to an accurate map of the world, or is this protected information? Are maps cheap or expensive? Coveted or common?

　
　
　

3. How accurate are the maps of the world? Are there fire-breathing dragons in the mountains and leviathans in the ocean? Does the edge just vanish into nothingness?

4. How were the maps created? Did someone sail across the ocean/climb a mountain? Did they use magic, or were there talking animals who shared the details?

___

5. How are places named in your world? Do inhabitants name places? Does a central location name everything? Do mapmakers name things?

___

6. Are there multiple names for the same place depending on who is talking? How much does this matter for your story? (Hello, Tolkien!)

___

7. What are the major cities readers need to know about? Where are they in relation to one another? What are those cities known for (reputation)? How much of this do your characters know? Do they have accurate information?

___

Part Two: The world is ... complicated

8. How big is a "big" city in your world? How many inhabitants are there (compared to the rest of the world)? Do your characters share this impression? What about minor cities? Where are they? What are they called? What are they known for?

_____
_____
_____

9. How about towns? How much do your characters know about the smaller places in your world? Are there small villages? Do they have names? Do your characters care about such places?

_____
_____
_____

10. What about the occasional cluster of inhabitants that live near the crossroad taverns? Is this considered a "town" or "village" in your world? What do your characters think as they experience these different places? How does their perception compare to the people who live in those places?

_____
_____
_____

11. Is there much trade between cities/towns? How does the trade take place—horseback/wagons/riverboats/shuttles/etc.? Do certain groups control trade in some way (we own the bridge, so we set the price for everything)? (See Section 3A for more questions on Economy.)

_____
_____
_____

The General Worldbuilding Guide

12. How much travel is common for the average person? Do people often travel to distant locations, or is this a strange occurrence for people in your world? How easy is it to travel? Think of Samwise Gamgee (in the movie version): "This is the farthest from home I've ever been." (See Section 3F for more questions about Travel.)

_____
_____
_____

13. How far is considered "far away" in your world? Was Shrek accurate in naming it "Away," "Far Away," and "Far, Far Away"? How are these distances shown on maps?

_____
_____
_____

14. Are there rivalries between places/people from different places? Do inhabitants have city/village/town pride in their hometowns? How do city dwellers feel about outsiders from other places in their city? How do these prejudices affect your story?

_____
_____
_____

15. How much is known by the average person about the rest of the cities/towns/villages in the world?

_____
_____
_____

Part Two: The world is ... complicated

A1. Earth-Variant Maps

1. How does your map compare to the map of the real world? Is your world the same relative size and shape?

   _____
   _____
   _____

2. Think about the politics that have gone into cartography in this world (i.e. Mercator projection). Has something similar happened in your world? Have maps been drawn to represent relative importance instead of geographic size?

   _____
   _____
   _____

3. Maps in this world have traditionally been made by travelers and explorers. Is this how maps are created in your world or do your inhabitants have another method?

   _____
   _____
   _____

4. How is the world commonly represented in your world? Our world uses flat maps and globes to convey geography—how do your inhabitants see these things?

___

5. Maps in our world can be unreliable and yet coveted. Do people make fake maps in your world (to deliberately mislead travelers)? Maps to buried treasure? Maps to secret cities and forgotten people? Are there keepers of map-lore that inhabitants must consult in order to know what lies beyond the mountains?

___

11. Known World Fun Activity

Think about some places that your main character would know about and jot down information about them in this chart!

Place Name			
Size			
Location (relative to where the story begins)			
Known for (trade/product)			
Reputation (Is this a safe place?)			
Who's in charge?			

Physical description (buildings, people, senses—smell/sound)			
Other known info			
Information your characters will learn after they get there			
Relevance to your story/plot			

Now is a good time to review the map you created for Activity 1 and 2. Is this still an accurate depiction of your world? Adjust as needed.

B. Government

1. Who is in charge of the town/city/country/world? What do the inhabitants of your world call their leaders—King, Czar, Supreme Leader, Baron, Chancellor, Lord, etc.?

_____
_____
_____

2. How is the world governed—democracy/monarchy/republic/oligarchy/etc.? How does the average person feel about this system of government? How do your characters feel about it? Why?

_____
_____
_____

3. How is the government structured and how does that structure affect your story? Are there local barons that the hero has vowed to take down? Is there a Supreme Emperor on another planet?

_____
_____
_____
_____

4. How involved is the average person in the government? Is ruling for a select few or are many people involved in the process?

___

5. Do citizens vote? Are all citizens allowed to vote or just certain ones? How does the voting system work?

___

6. Have there been rebellions against the government in the past? Why? What did people object to? What happened as a result? Is the current government the result of a rebellion?

___

7. If there was a rebellion (or many rebellions), was it a very long time ago or fresh in the minds of the people? How does the average person in the world feel about it? Are the rebels heroes or villains (and in whose eyes)?

___

Part Two: The world is ... complicated

8. What kind of fallout resulted from the rebellions? Were certain groups rewarded/punished? How? (Think about District 13 in *The Hunger Games*.)

_____
_____
_____

9. Are people happy or discontent with the current central government? How vocal are they about their feelings? How do inhabitants feel about the local government? Why?

_____
_____
_____

10. How do you become a ruler? Noble bloodline or strongest man in the room or most wealth or specific quality/ability—pull sword from stone/wield magic weapon?

_____
_____
_____

11. How do you join the governing body (if more than one person)? Can anyone join by running or are there specific qualifications? Are leaders elected or appointed?

_____
_____
_____

12. What qualities do the people look for in a ruler? Do they value experience or youth? (*Star Wars* had Naboo always ruled by children.)

_____
_____
_____

13. How involved is the government in the lives of the average person? Is it a distant thing that only certain people care about or is politics something that concerns most citizens?

_____
_____
_____

14. How does the government establish laws? Do people have any say in the laws (voting) or does a small group decide the rules for everyone? Do laws go through a committee?

_____
_____
_____

15. How are the laws enforced? Is there a government or police force to keep everyone in line? Does this force use the threat of violence or destruction? Is there a special class of citizens who enforce laws? How does the average person feel about this group? How do your characters feel about them?

_____
_____
_____

Part Two: The world is ... complicated

16. Can anyone join the enforcers? What's the process for joining (academy, trial by combat, etc.)? Is the law equally applied to everyone or do certain groups enjoy certain privileges?

_____
_____
_____

17. What happens if someone breaks the law? Prison/rehab/fines/exile/death? What are the penalties for common crimes—murder, theft, rape, kidnapping, assault? Are there debtor's prisons? How full are the prisons in this world? How common is crime? Do the people have a prison system to reform criminals? How does it work?

_____
_____
_____

18. Is there a death penalty? How does it work (hanging/burning/firing squad)? What crimes warrant the death penalty? Why?

_____
_____
_____

19. What happens if someone is accused of a crime? How does that process work? Is justice meted out fairly, or do other factors come into play? Do lawyers exist in your world?

_____
_____
_____

20. How do people feel about criminals after they serve their sentence? Are they marked somehow—brand/tattoo, paperwork, etc.? Can a former criminal reintegrate into society, or like Jean Valjean, do they need a new name and identity?

_____
_____
_____

21. Does the government provide any social services for people who need it? Is there a government-run tax-supported food pantry, medical care, transportation service, etc.?

_____
_____
_____

Part Two: The world is ... complicated

22. Are there government agencies that oversee the people's behavior other than the police? Does Child Protection Services exist? Will they take children into custody?

_____
_____
_____

23. What does the government do, if anything, about orphans?

_____
_____
_____

24. Where is the government located in your world—is it in a specific city, or does it move around?

_____
_____
_____

25. How much does the average person know about the government?

_____
_____
_____

B1.
Earth-Variant Government

1. How recognizable is the government in your story? Does it mimic real-world political systems that readers will know?

___

2. Does your story use popular figures of the day that readers may recognize (Hitler without naming him Hitler)? How have you changed these political figures for your story?

___

3. How much do you expect your readers to know about the government? How much do they need to know in order for the plot to make sense? Do they need to know that the crown goes to the entire male line of one brother before it bounces over to the entire male line of the next brother (so nephews become king before the next brother does)?

4. Why did you choose this government for your story? Why not another system?

_____

_____

_____

5. Does the government fit in the forefront or the background of your story? How much of this does your reader need to know in order for the story to function?

_____

_____

_____

12. Government Fun Activity

Take a moment to jot down some notes about the rules and rulers for the places your characters will go.

Place Name			
Ruler/ruling body			
Reputation of ruler			
How did they come to power?			
How much control do they have over this place?			
How do the locals feel about the ruler?			
Relevant laws to your story			
Do your characters have past history with these rulers?			

Part Two: The world is ... complicated

C. Society

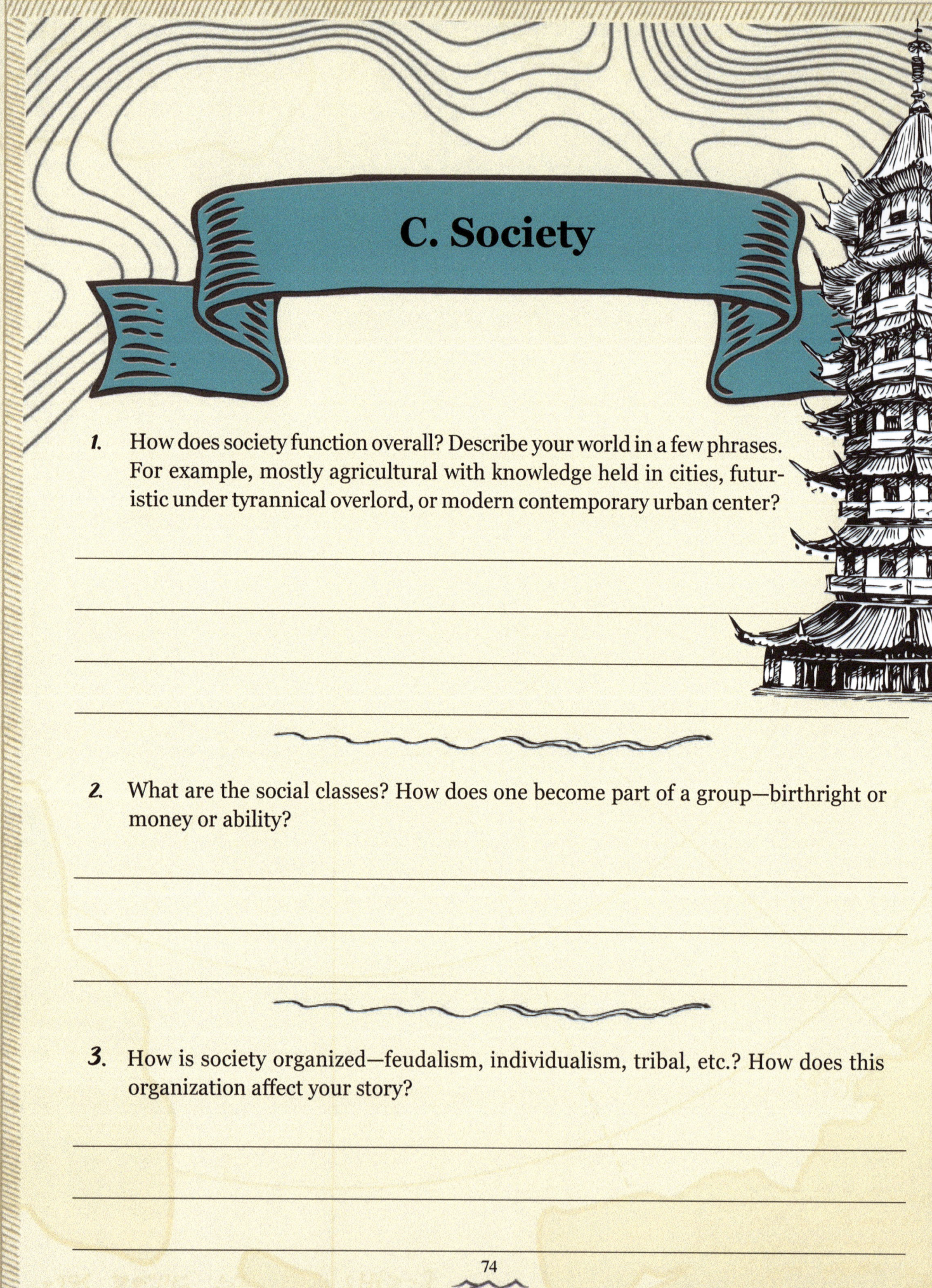

1. How does society function overall? Describe your world in a few phrases. For example, mostly agricultural with knowledge held in cities, futuristic under tyrannical overlord, or modern contemporary urban center?

_____
_____
_____
_____

2. What are the social classes? How does one become part of a group—birthright or money or ability?

_____
_____
_____

3. How is society organized—feudalism, individualism, tribal, etc.? How does this organization affect your story?

_____
_____
_____

4. Are there special names for different groups in society? Do certain skills group together? What brings the groups together? Are people chosen at birth like Jedi or stolen from parents like storm troopers or sent a letter like Harry Potter? What are the criteria that divide inhabitants—money/bloodline/location/etc.?

_____
_____
_____

5. Is there a huge difference between rich and poor? Is wealth evenly spread out among the inhabitants? Are financial resources something people in your world fight over?

_____
_____
_____

6. Is there a class that everyone hates? Why?

_____
_____
_____
_____

7. Do people envy the nobility? What perks do the upper class enjoy? Is it just food and physical comfort or are there special privileges (ease of travel, exotic items, etc.)? Can a person join the nobility? Is there any social mobility? Do inhabitants move up and down—why?

_____
_____
_____

8. How do people feel about those who move up/down socially? Is social mobility something to strive for or something forbidden? What can cause a shift in status?

_____
_____
_____

9. What behaviors are acceptable/expected from your inhabitants? What are things that everyone has in common? What do certain groups believe that varies from the general consensus?

_____
_____
_____

10. What behaviors/beliefs are taboo? Why? Is there a covenant regarding relationships? Sacred laws regarding food consumption? Words people cannot speak aloud? Were they always taboo, or did something happen to make them forbidden?

_____
_____
_____
_____

11. What happens to inhabitants who break taboos? Why does that happen? How often does this happen? How dire are the consequences?

_____
_____
_____
_____

12. What are common superstitions that your characters will encounter? Are black cats and the number 13 unlucky? Do people toss salt over a certain shoulder or avoid breaking mirrors at all costs? What beliefs bring people together in your world?

_____
_____
_____

13. Where did those superstitions come from? Do people remember? Were they the result of a specific incident or behavior patterns set down by the ancient ones or a new trend that never let go?

_____
_____
_____

14. How much has society changed in the last few years? Has there been a major shift in behavior/values? What happened? Do people want society to shift in some fundamental way? How? Why?

_____
_____
_____

15. How much does the average person know about the big picture when it comes to society?

_____
_____
_____

Part Two: The world is ... complicated

C1. Earth-Variant Society

1. How does your society reflect the one you are familiar with in this world? What aspects did you retain for your story? Why keep those?

___
___
___

2. In what ways have you altered your society in the story? Why did you make those changes? Did they help push the story forward, or is this the world you want for your characters?

___
___
___

3. Would your characters feel at home in the world you know? What behaviors would they recognize? What would seem strange to them?

___
___
___
___

4. What behaviors from this world that do not exist in their world would your characters embrace? Would your 14th century knight love driving a sports car? Would your sci-fi astronaut enjoy time on Twitter? Would your love interest like watching game shows? How would your characters fit into the world you know?

_____
_____
_____

5. What are some behaviors from this world that you want to bring into your story but can't for practical reasons? List them here, so you can let them go and stop trying to force it to work.

_____
_____
_____

13.
Society Fun Activity

It's time to layout your society from top to bottom! Who is at the top and why? Who lingers in the middle? Who's at the bottom?

Who is at the top?				
Who is in the middle?				
Who is at the bottom?				

D. Cultural Practices

1. What are the cultural practices of the people in your world? How are the cultural guidelines unique? Are they specific to different groups? In what way? (Do they brush their teeth with their toes? Do they leave their babies with strangers? Do they shave their heads before childbirth? Do they use distilled human remains to lengthen their lives like in *Jupiter Ascending*?)

   _____
   _____
   _____

2. How do different groups of people view one another and why? What is the power dynamic between different groups (gender, race, country, etc.)? Are men in charge of women or vice versa, or are they equal? Are certain races or nationalities seen in specific ways? (Women are subservient, Vikings are wild men, orcs are evil, Native Americans are noble savages, etc.).

   _____
   _____
   _____

3. What religions exist in your world? How do they function, and who follows them? How important is religion in this world—enough to fight wars over? (See Section 2E for more questions about Warfare.)

_____
_____
_____

4. Does slavery exist in your world? How does it work? Which group enslaves what other group? How do people become slaves, and how can they be freed? How do other cultures view those who practice slavery?

_____
_____
_____

5. What is considered a family unit in this world? How does the average person define "family"? What determines who runs a family unit? Is it the breadwinner, the oldest, the one born under a good sign?

_____
_____
_____

6. How does the average family unit live—parents and children or with grandparents and cousins? Is there a point where relatives are not considered family, but are still part of the community? Can you marry your third cousin twice removed in a small town where everyone comes from the same general bloodline?

_____
_____
_____

7. Are small or big families common in your world? At what point has one reached a "big" family? Is this a social status thing—do lower classes have fewer children while higher classes have many?

___

8. What is the general attitude toward birth control in your world? Is it available? Is it encouraged or frowned upon? Does abortion exist as a medical procedure or a concoction of plants? How do people view single parents?

___

9. At what age is an inhabitant considered an adult? What is the average life expectancy for your people? How does social status affect that projection? Do wealthier people live longer?

___

10. How is adulthood different from childhood? Is "childhood" a thing in your world or are children expected to behave like little adults from the time they can walk and communicate?

___

common child rearing practices among inhabitants? How are children [trea]ted in your world? How do parents discipline their children? Are [children] expected to work right away, or can they wait until they are older?

_____
_____
_____

12. What kind of stories are told to the children of your world? Is there a boogeyman? What are children taught to fear? To respect? Why?

_____
_____
_____

13. What kind of games do children play? Where do those games come from?

_____
_____
_____

14. What are some of the sports in your world? How are they played?

_____
_____
_____

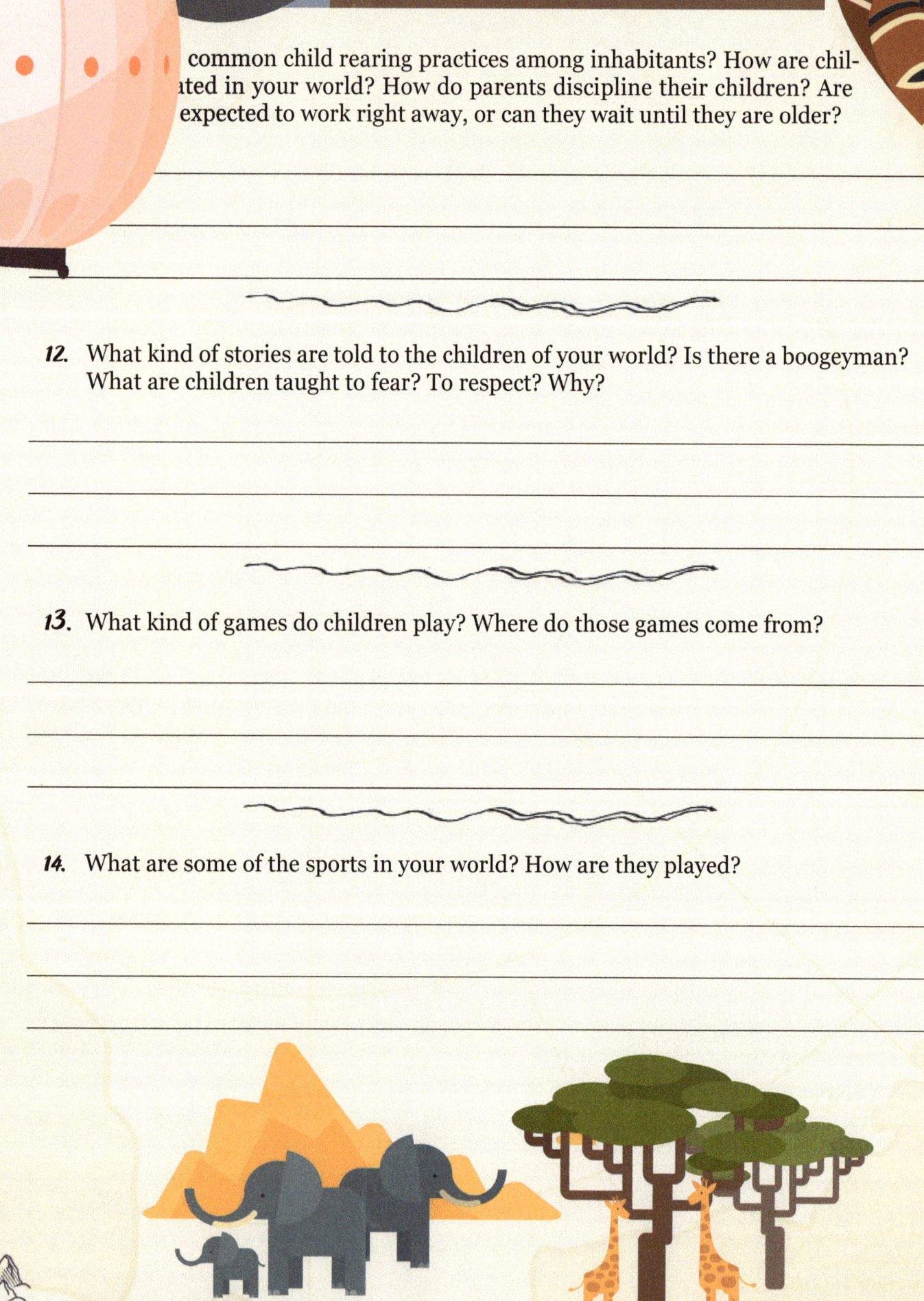

15. Are professional sports a thing in your world? Do people follow them as spectators, or would that be weird for them to think about? Who plays them, watches them, finances them, etc.?

_____
_____
_____

16. What is considered art in your world? Is it the traditional Humanities (painting, sculpture, music, literature, etc.), or is there more to it? Do people argue about what is "art"? Is art valued in this world or seen as a waste of time and energy? Is reading stories or listening to music a treasured moment or a lazy indulgence?

_____
_____
_____

17. What kind of music do people listen to or create? What instruments do they use? Is music written down for others to read later, or is it strictly an oral tradition?

_____
_____
_____

18. Are there writers in your world? Oral storytellers? What do people think about fiction—creating untrue stories? Is this a coveted career?

_____
_____
_____

19. Can artists in your world be self-taught, or do they need formal training? What does formal art training look like in your world—an academy/tutor/mentor?

_____
_____
_____

20. Can the average person in this world read? Are fiction/non-fiction books a thing, or are they oral stories, or both? How many books does the typical person in the world have at home? What kind of books would a person read—fiction, history, science?

_____
_____
_____

21. How do people relax in your world? What are some common hobbies? What activities would the average person do at home after the "major" work of the day is over—needlecraft, painting, sculpting, cooking, watching television?

_____
_____
_____

22. Is the schedule of the average person set by sunlight and everyone goes to sleep at sunset, or do people stay up after dark to do things? Is non-natural light available? How is the average day divided into work and play? (See Section 3E for more questions about Technology.)

_____
_____
_____

23. Are there major holidays in your world? What are they? Where did they come from? How do inhabitants celebrate important days throughout the year? Do people celebrate equinoxes/solstices? Are certain days more important than others? (See Section 4D for more questions about Calendars.)

_____
_____
_____

24. How do inhabitants keep track of birthdays? Are they celebrated? Do birthdays involve cake and presents or something else? (Hobbits give away presents on their birthday.)

_____
_____
_____

25. What are common hygiene practices for the people? Do they bathe every day, wear perfume, wash their clothes often? Is there an industry of products around hygiene (hair, body wash, soap, make-up, etc.)?

_____
_____
_____

26. How much food does the average person have in their home? Is it common for people to make dinner at home, or do they grab food elsewhere? Is food delivery a thing in this world (Doordash, Uber eats, etc.)?

_____
_____
_____

27. What are some popular foods that are unique to your world? What is considered a lavish meal, an afternoon snack, a poor-man's-breakfast?
_____
_____
_____

28. Is food preserved in some way, or is it all fresh? Do people store food for the winter because they must supply it themselves, or is it always available?
_____
_____
_____

29. What do the inhabitants of your world celebrate (birth, graduation, new cars)?
_____
_____
_____

30. What do they grieve (war, famine, death of a loved one)? What do they fear (spiders, zombies, pandemic)?
_____
_____
_____

31. What do they love (other people, satisfying pens, great advice)?
_____
_____
_____

32. Do people have pets? What is considered a normal pet in your world? Where is the line between a pet and a food source?

___

33. What do people value? What is considered beautiful or handsome? What facial/body features are prized right now?

___

34. Are certain traditions prized more than others? What practices are looked down on by most people?

___

35. How much does the average person know about the cultural practices of other people?

D1. Earth-Variant Cultural Practices

1. Which cultures from this world have you replicated in your world? What made you choose them and not a different one (Northern Ireland 1970 vs Japan 1590 vs US 1692)?

___
___
___
___

2. What cultural practices do you assume your readers are familiar with? Will they need some background on celebrating Christmas, tweeting an image, surviving middle school dances, graduating college?

___
___
___
___

3. What cultural practices do you plan to introduce to your readers as something they might not know much about? Why did you choose those behaviors and not others?

___
___
___
___

4. Do you plan to use your story to make a comment on society? How will your use of cultural practices affect that underlying message?

_____
_____
_____

5. Are you shifting a common cultural practice to present it in a new light for your readers? How and why?

_____
_____
_____

14. Culture Fun Activity

Take a moment and create cultural practices/beliefs that are unique to your world.

- What is a specific cultural practice or belief that affects the plot of your story? Where did this practice come from and why? How does it affect your characters?

  _____
  _____
  _____
  _____

- List three games that the children in your world play. What are the rules? How does one "win" the game? Where did the game come from? How seriously do the players take the game and the rules?

  _____
  _____
  _____
  _____

- List three sports that are common in your world. How are they played? How do your characters feel about these sports? Will your hero join in a goblin version of rugby?

  _____
  _____
  _____
  _____

- Describe three popular works of art that the people in your world would recognize (painting: *Mona Lisa*, music: Beethoven's 5th, book: *War and Peace*). They don't have to know it intimately—just be aware of it as a thing in their world.

- What are the top five jobs in your world? What makes them the top five (most lucrative, most fulfilling, most needed)?

- Write down two major holidays that affect your plot and characters. When do they occur, and how are they celebrated?

- Describe a typical birthday celebration in your world. Do people sing a specific song, eat cake, and give presents? Do they give away presents like hobbits? How specific are these practices to specific areas? Americans are often surprised by the Australian version of the "happy birthday" song.

- Describe common dishes your characters may encounter. What food do they enjoy, crave, miss? What food do they dislike, hate, avoid?

  _____
  _____
  _____
  _____

E. Warfare

1. How are wars fought in your world? Do people fight with swords on horseback or with lasers in ships?

2. What are some major conflicts that your characters would know about? What happened and how does it affect your story?

3. How involved is the average person in wars? Do they have their children conscripted to fight in the holy war, or is there fighting in some distant land that has been going on forever?

4. Are the people living under threat all the time (under siege), or is the world relatively peaceful? How was that peace attained?

_____

_____

_____

5. What is the command structure for war? Who can declare war? What happens next? Is it decided by single combat, nuclear bombs, or economic destruction?

_____

_____

_____

6. Is there a standing military ready to fight? Who actually goes to war in that command structure? Do the commanders fight alongside their troops or issue orders from a safe bunker? In Dee Lambert's *Rydan*, the prince fights alongside his men (and even faces a dragon!).

_____

_____

_____

7. How is the military formed? Do people volunteer, does everyone have to join, or are people drafted during wartime? How does the average person feel about the military?

_____

_____

_____

8. Can people leave the army if they want to? Is service a lifelong commitment or a voluntary choice? How do people (veterans and non-veterans) view those who no longer serve?

___

9. Does the military take care of its wounded troops after the fighting is over? How well are troops treated when the war is over?

___

10. How satisfied are those who serve in the military? Are they happy to be there or resentful of having to fight?

___

11. How do troops communicate on the battlefield? Do they use semaphores, radios, or satellites?

___

12. How are armies supplied during battle? How does the supply chain fit into strategic planning for warfare? Are wagon trains or convoys with supplies a target? Where do those extra wartime supplies come from? Does the country mobilize to create what is needed (everyone works in the munitions factory), or do outside corporations step in to offer support?

_____
_____
_____

13. Why have wars occurred in your world? What were they fought over—land, power, preemptive, love? Are these major battles with long-standing effects felt for decades or minor skirmishes along the river that are forgotten in a month or so?

_____
_____
_____

14. Does the average person in your world know how to defend themselves in a fight? Is combat common or rare? Do people carry weapons?

_____
_____
_____

15. How much does the average person in your world know about warfare?

_____
_____
_____

E1. Earth-Variant Warfare

1. How much do your fictional wars reflect actual wars in human history?

___

2. How much background will your readers need to understand the point you are making by including the war? You don't want your story to turn into a history textbook (though maybe you can write that one after you finish this one!), so decide how much you need to share to move your story forward.

___

3. What details about warfare will you emphasize in your story (methods, geography, technology, aftereffects, etc.)? How do these details affect the story you are telling? How have your characters been affected by warfare?

___

4. How much research have you done on warfare? If war is going to be a major component in your story, you should probably do a little more than watch a movie or two and skim an article online. Readers respond to realism—even in fictional worlds. Do your homework and give readers the experience they deserve.

_____

_____

_____

5. Are you altering the circumstances of a real war (alternate history)? What details are you keeping and which will shift for your story?

_____

_____

_____

15. Warfare Fun Activity

Think about the history of your world. Take a moment to jot down some notes about important wars that your characters would know about.

Name of war				
Parties involved				
Length of fighting				
Causes for war				

Part Two: The world is ... complicated

Places of note (major battles, assassination attempts, etc.)				
Methods used (swords, guns, airplanes, trenches, etc.)				
Effects on your storyline				

F. Appearance

1. What do your inhabitants look like? Describe the different people in your world.

   _____
   _____
   _____

2. What kind of clothing do your inhabitants wear? Describe a "typical" person your characters will encounter.

   _____
   _____
   _____

3. Do certain styles have special significance? What do they mean to those wearing them, to those seeing the garments? Is clothing divided along gender lines? In what way? Describe the different styles. What does clothing style reveal about the people who live in this world?

   _____
   _____
   _____
   _____

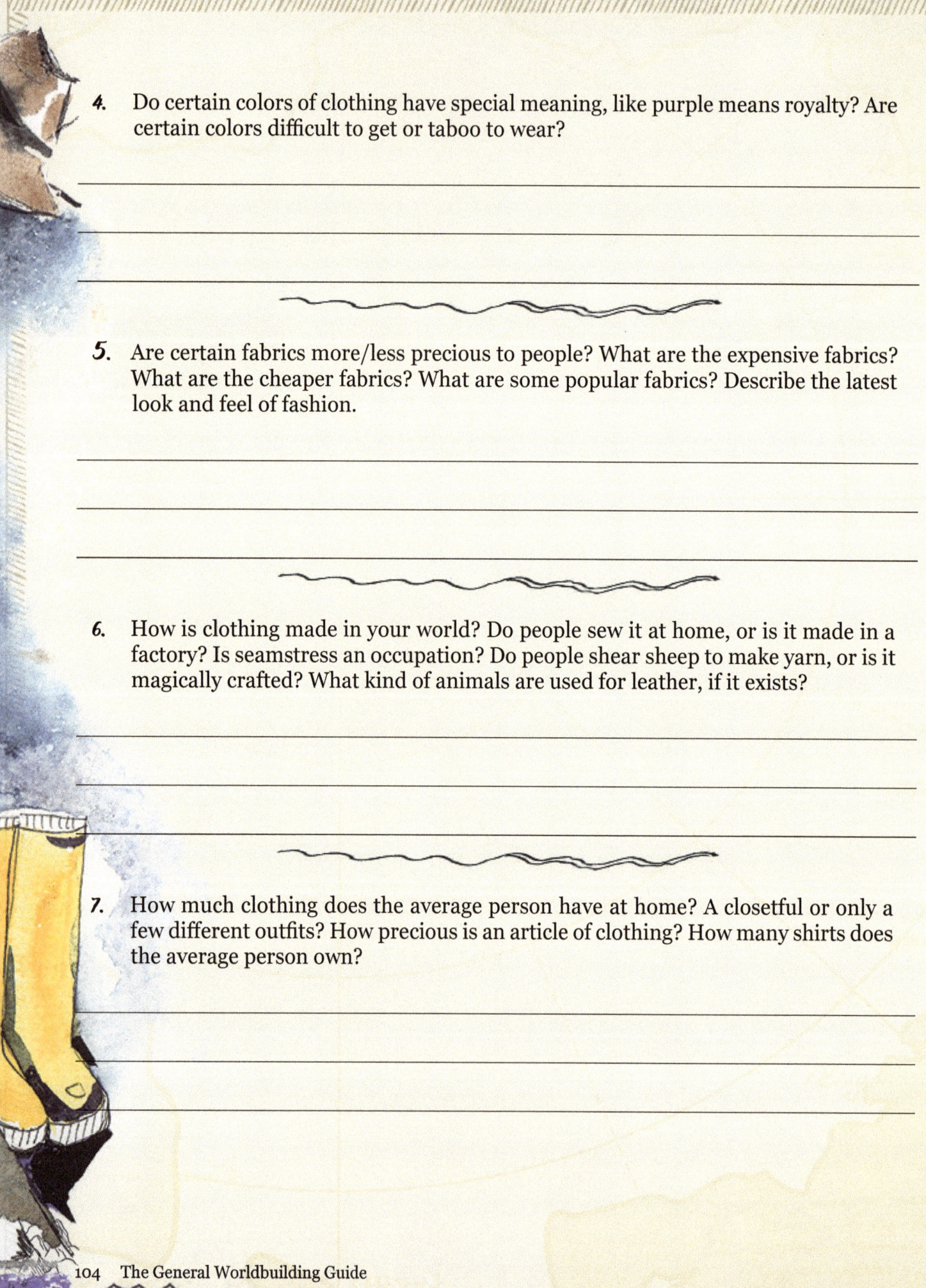

4. Do certain colors of clothing have special meaning, like purple means royalty? Are certain colors difficult to get or taboo to wear?

_____

_____

_____

5. Are certain fabrics more/less precious to people? What are the expensive fabrics? What are the cheaper fabrics? What are some popular fabrics? Describe the latest look and feel of fashion.

_____

_____

_____

6. How is clothing made in your world? Do people sew it at home, or is it made in a factory? Is seamstress an occupation? Do people shear sheep to make yarn, or is it magically crafted? What kind of animals are used for leather, if it exists?

_____

_____

_____

7. How much clothing does the average person have at home? A closetful or only a few different outfits? How precious is an article of clothing? How many shirts does the average person own?

_____

_____

_____

8. Do people wear many layers or just one? Are underclothes a thing? Do women wear corsets and skirt cages or shifts and belts?

___

9. What is the general attitude toward nudity? Public nudity? Are there laws about this? How are they enforced? What happens if someone breaks the law?

___

10. How do people accessorize their outfits? Is jewelry common or precious? What does jewelry look like?

___

11. Do certain types of jewelry have special significance? How is jewelry made? Are certain stones precious? Do specific items hold special meaning (rings on left ring finger = married)?

___

12. How do people wear their hair? Do certain styles have special meaning (braids = unmarried, etc.)?

___

13. Can you tell a person's social status by their appearance? How?

___

14. Is there a fashion center in this world, like Paris or Milan, that others defer to when choosing the newest fashions?

___

15. How much does the average person know about clothing?

___

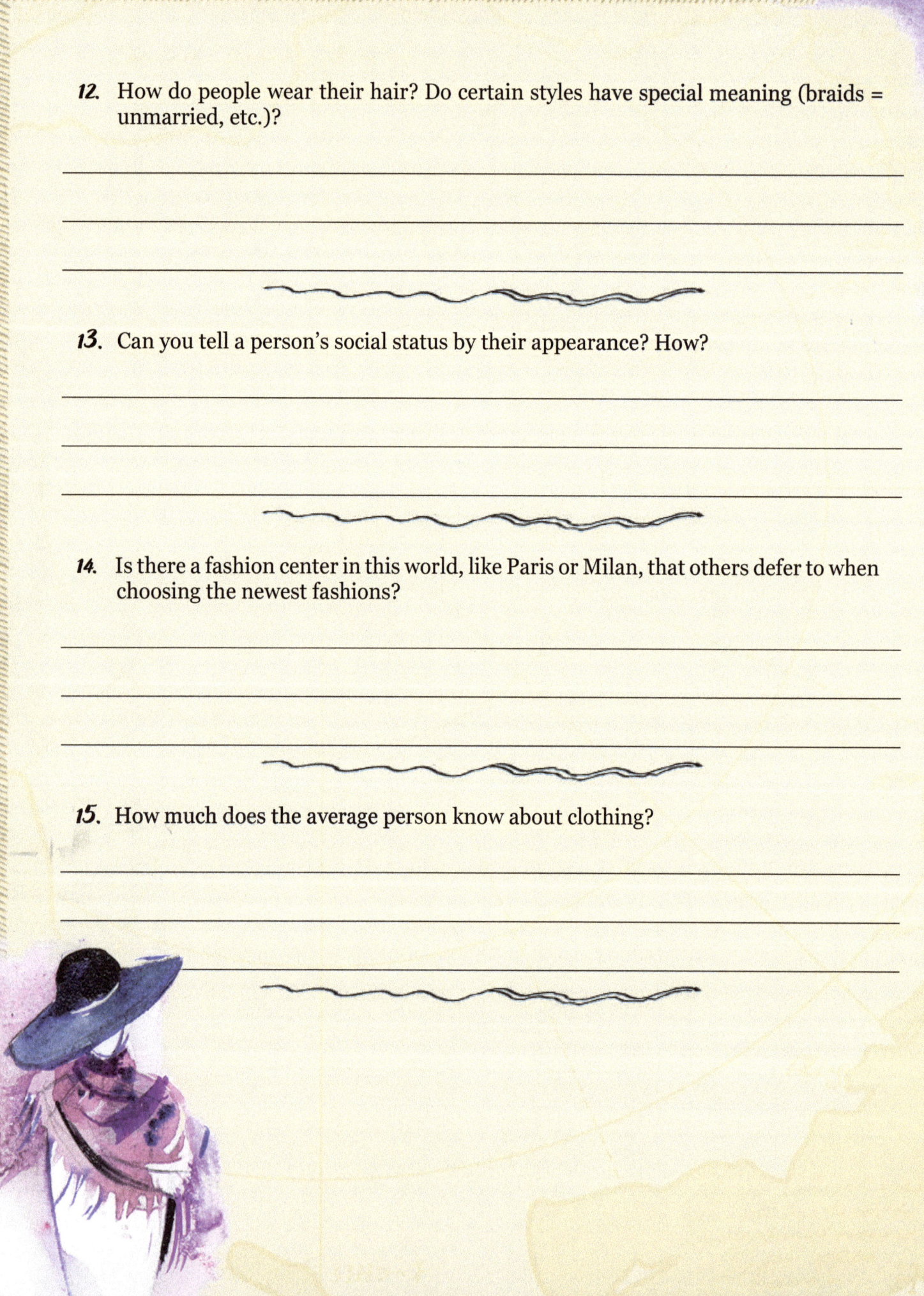

F1. Earth-Variant Appearance

(*This section title belongs in a science fiction novel.)

1. How much of your story depicts characters recognizable by your readers? Are you using stereotypical descriptions for your characters?

   _____
   _____
   _____

2. Consider the real-world implications of the appearance of your characters. How would those people be perceived in the world today? Is that how you want your readers to think about them?

   _____
   _____
   _____

3. In what ways have you shifted traditional appearances for your story? Why did you choose to change those details and not others?

   _____
   _____
   _____

4. How much can be discerned about your characters by their appearance? Do they fit the expectations of those who see them, or do they break the rules?

_____

_____

_____

_____

5. How will the appearance of your characters shift over the course of your story, if at all? Will they begin with more traditionally recognizable appearances and slowly shift into something else?

_____

_____

_____

_____

16.
Clothing Fun Activity: Dress Your Characters

What do your characters *wear* and what does it signify to them? If you are artistically inclined, draw your main characters! If you are not gifted in that area, find pictures online of what your characters look like. Build a Pinterest board of people and places for each story (readers **LOVE** seeing a Pinterest board for a world they are reading).

Name	Description of Clothing/Jewelry	Significance of Items

Part Two: The world is ... complicated

17. Appearance Fun Activity: Dress Your Side Characters

Now it's time for the minor characters. What do the people your characters encounter look like? Take a moment to create five stock character appearances that you can use in the background of important scenes.

Character/Location/Relevance: Who is this person and where do your characters encounter them?	Clothing? Describe the outfit the person is wearing.	Special Features (jewelry, hairstyle, fancy gloves, etc.) and any known significance to characters	Physical Traits (height/weight/hair/eyes/skin, etc.)	Notable Quality, if any (random thought a character may have about this person?)

Part Two: The world is … complicated

Build Your World Activities

18. Character Culture Study

It's time to think about your characters! For each *main character*, take a moment to write down the following information:

- What does this character value above everything else in the world (honor, love, justice, their mother's ring, a special pair of blue boots)?

_____
_____
_____
_____

- What are three core cultural beliefs this character holds dear that will be challenged during your story?

_____
_____
_____
_____

- What are three cultural practices that this character will display during your story (pray before meals, bless someone after sneezing, knock on wood)?

_____
_____
_____
_____

- What are some cultural conflicts that will affect your story? Are they based on misunderstandings? Different values? Perception or preconceived notions?

_____
_____
_____
_____

19. FIGHT!

Most stories have some kind of **CONFLICT**—and that interaction may involve a physical altercation. Think about how each of your characters fight. Consider these questions for each character who will get involved in a fight:

- What is this character's weapon of choice?

  _____
  _____
  _____
  _____
  _____

- How skilled are they with the weapon?

  _____
  _____
  _____
  _____
  _____

- How did they get that skilled? Where/when/how/why did they train?

  _____
  _____
  _____
  _____
  _____

- Jot down an anecdote from their training days—what happened the first time they picked up a morning star?

_____
_____
_____
_____
_____

- What weapon will they use in extremity (They don't like it, but they know how to use it)? What do they dislike about it? Why?

_____
_____
_____
_____
_____
_____

- What weapon do they hate and refuse to use? Why? Tell that story! Did they hit themselves in the face with a whip the first time they picked it up and swore to never use one again?

_____
_____
_____
_____

- Special abilities time—what can this character do that is unique to them? How does this ability factor into the story?

_____
_____
_____
_____

Build Your World Activities

- What is this character's best fighting style/technique? Under what circumstances will they always win?

_____

_____

_____

_____

- What is this character's fighting weakness? Under what circumstances will they fail?

_____

_____

_____

_____

- Describe the first fight this character won—what happened?

_____

_____

_____

_____

- Describe the first fight this character lost—what happened?

_____

_____

_____

_____

- What is this character's fighting philosophy? Float like a butterfly–sting like a bee?

_____
_____
_____
_____

20.
Your Story Time: The World is ... Complicated

It's time to take notes on how this *information* will affect the story you have in mind. It's okay if the answer to some of these questions is "**ABSOLUTELY NOTHING AT ALL!**" Or "I don't know!" Even if this information doesn't come into play directly, it's still good to have it in the back of your mind (in case an eager reader writes an email asking about it one day—you'll have a ready reply!).

1. You've created a map for the events of your world. How does this visualization help you imagine your story?

   _____
   _____
   _____

2. You've considered how the government functions in your world. How will this organization affect the events in your story?

   _____
   _____
   _____

3. You've thought about how your society is made up. How will these social restrictions and guidelines come up in your story?

   _____
   _____
   _____

4. You've detailed cultural practices for your world. How will these behaviors affect the plot of your story (cause confusion, start conflict, generate affection, forge bonds, etc.)?

_____
_____
_____

5. You've thought about how warfare and character fighting styles work in your world. What part will fighting play in your story?

_____
_____
_____
_____

6. You've painted the appearance of the inhabitants in your world. How will you keep track of the appearance of your main characters so they don't randomly have a different color shirt on?

_____
_____
_____

USE THIS SPACE TO JOT DOWN OTHER IDEAS THAT THIS SECTION HAS SPARKED—THEY MAY BE USEFUL AT SOME POINT!

Part Three: But why did they do that?

This part continues working on your world, but with a focus on different areas that may motivate the characters and propel the events in your story. Part Three addresses Economy, Education, Relationships, Communication, Technology, Travel, and Health and Wellness.

A. Economy

1. How would you describe the economic system in your world (capitalism, communism, socialism, bartering, etc.)?

_____

_____

_____

2. Do people study the economy as a subject in this world? Are there books or discussions about the way goods are exchanged?

_____

_____

_____

3. What is considered "work" in your world? How do inhabitants feel about working? Is having a job a mark of honor or shame? Are certain jobs considered virtuous? Contemptible? Which ones? Why?

_____

_____

_____

4. Is taking care of children and the household considered "work"? If so, how is it compensated?

_____

_____

_____

5. How does money work in the world (coins/paper/jewels/goods)? Jot down your monetary system and the modern equivalent so that you can keep it organized.

_____

_____

_____

6. How is the money distributed in the world? Does the average person have enough to survive? Are loans for money a thing, or do people barter for goods and services? Can a piece of paper count for money in any way (a bill of sale, IOU)?

_____

_____

_____

7. Do people hoard certain things? What are they, and why do they have value?

_____

_____

_____

Part Three: But why did they do that

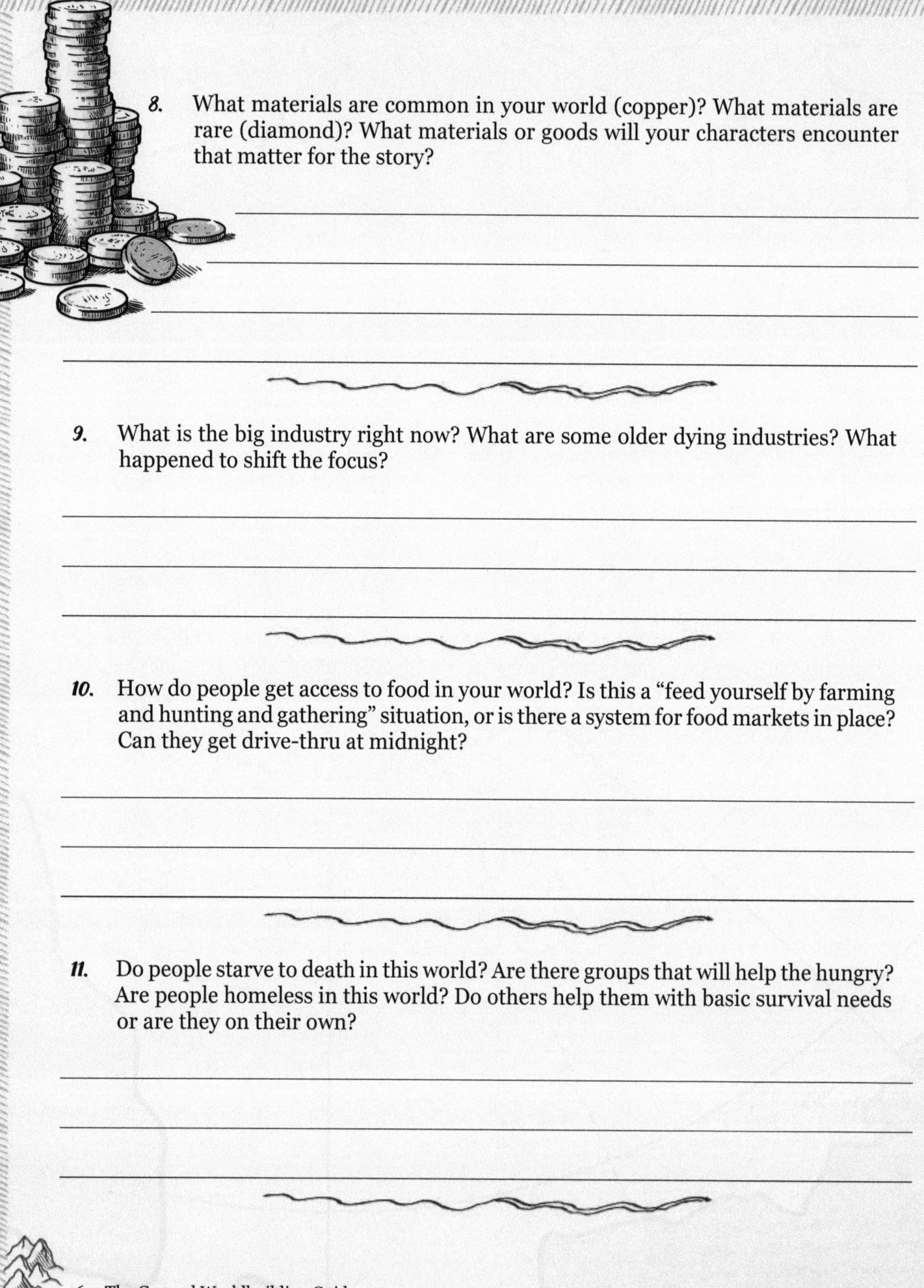

8. What materials are common in your world (copper)? What materials are rare (diamond)? What materials or goods will your characters encounter that matter for the story?

___

9. What is the big industry right now? What are some older dying industries? What happened to shift the focus?

___

10. How do people get access to food in your world? Is this a "feed yourself by farming and hunting and gathering" situation, or is there a system for food markets in place? Can they get drive-thru at midnight?

___

11. Do people starve to death in this world? Are there groups that will help the hungry? Are people homeless in this world? Do others help them with basic survival needs or are they on their own?

___

12. Do people pay a tax to an entity in exchange for certain public services? Are there police or firefighters or well-maintained roads? Is it everyone for themselves?

___
___
___

13. What is considered a "lot" of money to the average person? What is a tiny amount of money? How much money does the average person make in a year? Are people paid in chunks or weekly?

___
___
___

14. How do people show their wealth or status (clothing, accessories, hairstyle, etc.)? What is your world's equivalent to a Brooks Brothers suit or a Prada bag?

___
___
___

15. How much does the average person know about the workings of the economy?

___
___
___
___

A1. Earth-Variant Economy

1. What economic system from this world also exists in your world? Why did you choose it and not something else? How does it affect your plot or character motivation?

_____
_____
_____

2. How much of the current economic climate have you included in your world? Are characters worried about similar issues (property values, rising taxes, shady business practices, etc.)?

_____
_____
_____

3. How important is the economic standing of your characters to your story? Do they need to hold down a job in order to stay in their homes, or does money not come up in your story at all? Why did you set up the story this way?

_____
_____
_____

4. How much research did you do to reliably portray an economic lifestyle that is not reflective of your own? If you mention the cost of items or how much money is required to live comfortably, how recent or accurate are those figures?

_____
_____
_____
_____

5. Is your story ultimately upholding the current economic status of the characters or changing it? Why did you choose to treat economic status this way in your story?

_____
_____
_____
_____

Part Three: But why did they do that

21.
Economy Fun Activity

Lay out your monetary system! What is the equivalent to the following amounts? What can a person buy with these amounts?

Amount	Equivalent in your currency	What can this buy?
$.01		
$.05		
$.10		
$.25		
$.50		
$1.00		
$2.00		
$5.00		
$10.00		
$20.00		
$50.00		
$100.00		
$500.00		
$1,000.00		
$5,000.00		
$10,000.00		
$50,000.00		
$100,000.00		
$500,000.00		
$1,000,000.00		
$5,000,000.00		
$500,000,000.00		
$1,000,000,000.00		

The General Worldbuilding Guide

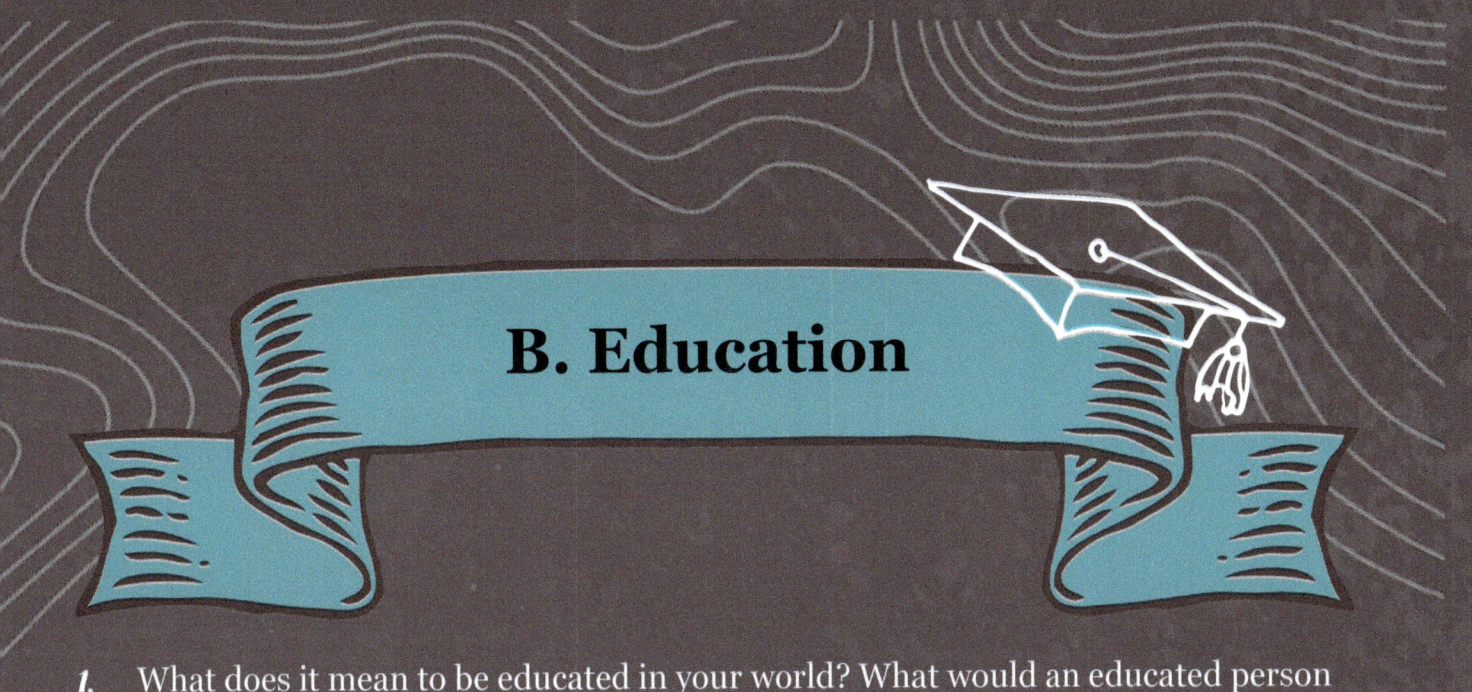

B. Education

1. What does it mean to be educated in your world? What would an educated person know that an uneducated one would not?

   _____
   _____
   _____

2. Are there public schools? Is school compulsory? Does everyone have to go to school? Are there private schools? Religious schools? How does a person learn things in your world? Are they trained at home by family? Who can go to school? Who cannot? Is it reserved for certain classes/people/families/locations?

   _____
   _____
   _____

3. How is the education system organized? How many levels of schooling are there? Who oversees this system? Is it specific to parts of the world or standardized everywhere (Common Core)?

   _____
   _____
   _____

4. Are there lifelong scholars? How does the rest of society view them? What do they study for a lifetime? Do they write down their findings and lecture to crowds, or do they hoard their knowledge?

___

5. Are there trade schools, or do people learn from an individual tradesperson? What are considered desirable trades? Why? What are undesirable trades?

___

6. How are educators viewed by the general public? Is teaching an honorable profession? Are educators paid well? What is required for one to become a teacher? Are there schools that train educators? Or is having knowledge/skills enough? Can anyone become a teacher?

___

7. What do students learn in school—skills, facts, or both? How are they assessed (OWLs, SATs, Divergence testing, trial by fire)?

___

8. Does graduation have any significance? How do people view this milestone? When does it happen (elementary school, middle school, high school, college, post-grad)?

9. Do inhabitants need official paperwork to prove their education, or do others trust their word? How is the paperwork stored or shared if it is required? Do people forge these?

10. Where is the knowledge in your world kept? Are libraries a thing? Is knowledge hoarded or shared with the people? How is information stored—books, data drives, communal memories?

11. Are there major schools that everyone knows about? Are there secret schools that only certain people know about? Why? What are they?

Part Three: But why did they do that

12. What does an average school day look like in your world? Break this down by age, if that's how your world works. Do people stay at home and attend school during the day, or do they go away to school for months at a time (or both, depending on economic situation)?

_____
_____
_____

13. What are the requirements to get into certain schools? How are students assessed and on what grounds? What is a "good" school?

_____
_____
_____

14. How do people view the educated? How do they view the uneducated?

_____
_____
_____

15. How much does the average person know about the educational system in your world?

_____
_____
_____

B1.
Earth-Variant Education

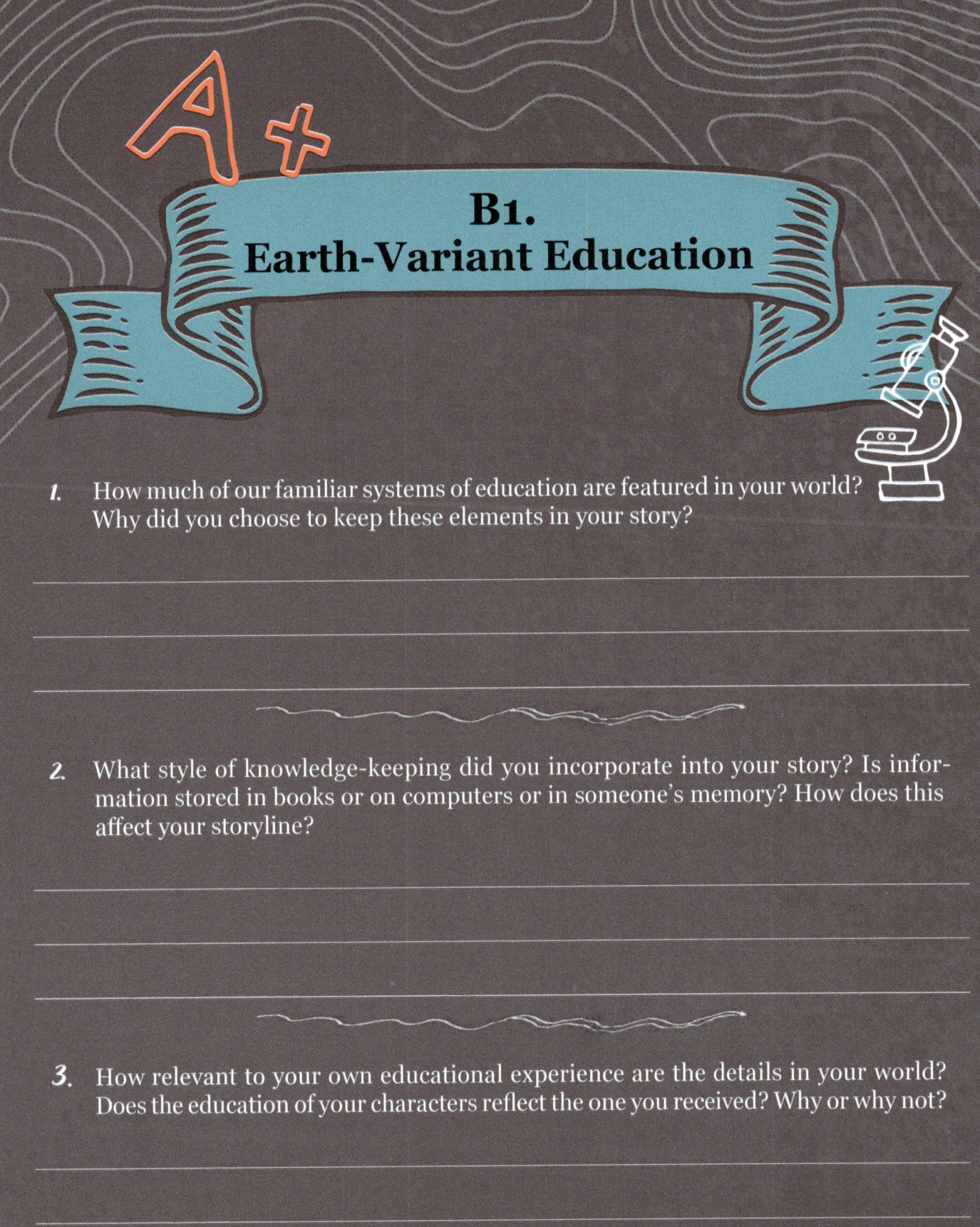

1. How much of our familiar systems of education are featured in your world? Why did you choose to keep these elements in your story?

2. What style of knowledge-keeping did you incorporate into your story? Is information stored in books or on computers or in someone's memory? How does this affect your storyline?

3. How relevant to your own educational experience are the details in your world? Does the education of your characters reflect the one you received? Why or why not?

4. Is your story following a popular trope (monster academy, magic school, etc.)? How much of the real-world is folded into your version of this common story? What aspects of the school experience have you altered and why?

_____
_____
_____

5. How important is the idea of education in your story? How important is the idea of education to you?

_____
_____
_____

22.
Education Fun Activity

Think about what a typical student in your world would learn about and how.

- What subjects are studied?
___
___
___
___

- Create textbook titles for your classes (*Hogwarts: A History*).
___
___
___
___

- Who are the important figures that your students learn about?
___
___
___
___

- What are important dates students might need to know?
___
___
___
___
___

Part Three: But why did they do that

What are scientific theories that are unique to your world?

_____
_____
_____

- Create some works of art (music, painting, sculpture, etc.) for your students to study.

_____
_____
_____

- How does math work in your world? Are the areas of study the same (fractions, polynomials, trigonometry, algebra, calculus, etc.)?

_____
_____
_____

- What areas of study are unique to your world (alchemy, quantum mechanics, ethical robotics, etc.)?

_____
_____
_____

- What days/times are those classes? How does the student schedule work?

_____
_____
_____

- What does a typical school look like? Are there tables and chairs, interactive desk surfaces, alchemical labs, rows of computers?

_____
_____
_____

C. Relationships

1. What does the average relationship look like in your world? Describe the typical romantic relationship.

   _____
   _____
   _____

2. What does an atypical romantic relationship in your world look like? Describe a relationship that exists but would surprise others.

   _____
   _____
   _____

3. Is gender the deciding factor for one's role in the relationship? How does gender present in your world? How are genders defined in your world (if gender is the social expectations associated with one's assumed sex, while sex is the biological determination using physical attributes)?

   _____
   _____
   _____
   _____

4. How many sexes exist in your world? Are there same-sex relationships? How does society view same-sex couples? In *Prince's Priest* by VC Willis, the scandal is that the relationship is between a vampire prince and a human priest. The fact that they are both men is an expected option in that world.

___

5. How do people feel about relationships between classes? What about relationships between races? How does the average person feel about people from different places being in a relationship?

___

6. How does a typical relationship progress? Describe the usual steps of a courtship (meeting, wooing, dating, flowers, sex, meeting families, moving in together, proposal, marriage, family, children, etc.).

___

7. Do people choose their partners or are relationships arranged by family members? Are arranged marriages the norm? Are they outdated or outlawed? If they are a thing, how do families determine a fitting suitor?

___

8. How do couples introduce prospective partners to their families? Is this an important step in the courtship process or just a casual affair?

___

9. Do couples live together (before/after marriage)? How does society feel about those who break this expectation one way or another?

___

10. Do couples get married, or does cohabitation mean they are an official relationship? Which relationships are recognized as official by the government? Does marriage matter, or is it just a minor bit of paperwork?

___

11. What does a typical wedding ceremony look like? Who attends? Who speaks and what do they say? Does someone need to vouch for the couple or forever hold their peace?

___

Part Three: But why did they do that

12. Do couples need permission to marry? From whom? Is there a waiting period, or can people get married right away?

___

13. Do people elope to Vegas or run away to be together? How does society feel about this behavior? Is it cute or romantic, juvenile or crazy?

___

14. Do people change their name when they get married? Is the new member fully embraced by the partner's family? (You're a Jones now!)

___

15. Is there a physical sign that shows a person is married (ring, hairstyle, article of clothing, etc.)? Can someone tell at a glance if a person is in a committed relationship or not?

16. Do couples marry for love? Convenience? A combination of both? Why do most couples pair up?

___

17. Can anyone marry anyone, or are there rules? Who establishes these rules? What happens to those who break the rules? Are they ostracized like Anna Karenina or forgiven like Count Vronsky?

___

18. What are the rules regarding marriage? Who established them? Why?

___

19. Is marriage about procreation and children and continuing the family name? How does society feel about childless couples? What is the general view on couples having children?

___

20. In terms of children, do couples value one sex over another (boys over girls)? How about twins or triplets, etc.? Are such children a blessing by the gods or a curse?

___

21. This will come up again in the Technology section under medicine, but consider the maternal mortality rate during childbirth in your world. Is childbirth a dangerous proposition for women in your world? (If only women can give birth.)

___

22. Are relationships limited to two people or do people support multiple partners in relationships? How does society view thruples/poly-groups? In *Signs of Affection* by Lynn Chantale, the main character courts a love interest who practices polyamory.

___

23. How does the average person define love in your world?

24. Is love something that happens to a person (over which there is no control)? Do people fall in love like they fall off a cliff? Is love a conscious decision made by a person? Can a person choose to fall in love?

25. Is love an expectation in relationships? Or is being part of a relationship more commonly a matter of convenience and love is found elsewhere?

26. How do people view adultery? How do people view emotional affairs? Physical affairs? Where is the line when a relationship has become adulterous (a glance, a stolen kiss, a long hug, sex)?

27. Are there established punishments for breaking a vow to a partner? How are they enforced? Are they different depending on who has committed the offense (women are killed, men are chastised)?

28. Is love predetermined by an outside force? By what/whom? Are certain lovers fated to be together in your world?

___

29. Is there a deity of love? Who is it? What powers do they have? How do people view this deity? How much control does a love deity have over the inhabitants?

___

30. Are there love potions/love spells in your world? How do such things work? How long does a love potion/spell last? What are the long-term effects of a love potion? (Are the children of such unions born unable to love like Voldemort?)

___

31. Do people believe in love at first sight? How do people feel about such relationships?

32. Is love an acceptable excuse for irrational behavior? Do people excuse "crazy" behavior on account of love?

___

33. Does love have physical symptoms? Can others see that a person is in love?

___

34. Are the majority of the inhabitants romantics or cynics when it comes to love? What do your characters think about this?

___

35. What does the average person think about relationships in your world?

___

Part Three: But why did they do that

C1. Earth-Variant Relationships

1. What kinds of familiar relationships are you featuring in your story? Why did you choose those and not others?

_____
_____
_____

2. What new types of relationships appear in your story? How are they different from traditional real-world connections?

_____
_____
_____

3. How much of the relationships depicted in your story are a reflection of your own experiences? What elements did you add to the relationships and why?

_____
_____
_____

4. How important are relationships in your story? Do they reflect real-world behavior, or are they exaggerated in some way? If so, how and why?

_____
_____
_____

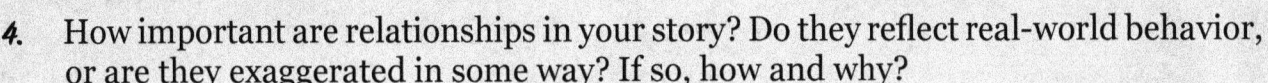

5. If your story were turned into a film, what category would Netflix put it under: romance, romantic comedy, drama, horror, etc.? How much of the distinction is based on the types of relationships you include in your story?

_____
_____
_____

23. Relationships Fun Activity: What is love?

How do your characters define *romantic love*? Use the following chart to jot down their thoughts on love in general.

Name			
Love at first sight?			
Love is a choice?			
Love is a physical reaction/ body function?			

There is someone out there for everyone (or more than one someones).			
Love is worth dying for/ killing for.			
Love is....			
Their ideal lover is...			

Part Three: But why did they do that   151

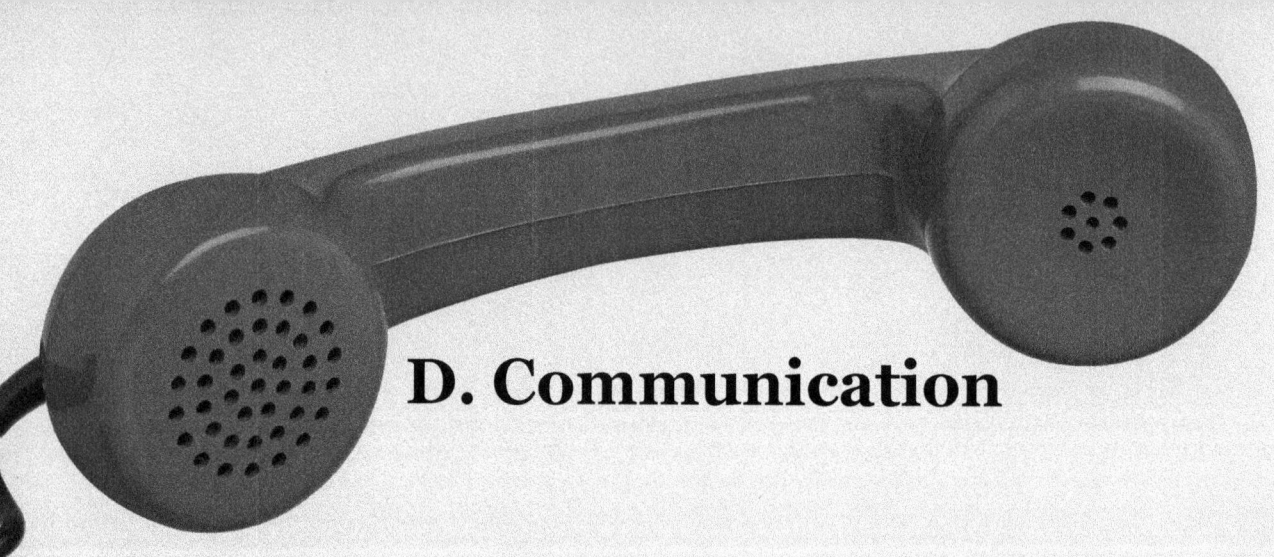

D. Communication

1. How do people send messages to one another in your world? Do they send riders on horses? Roll up messages on pigeon legs? Send letters with owls? Send texts with phones? Send thoughts through telepathy?

2. Is there technology to send messages—telegraph, telegram, telephone? Are there Klax machines to transmit messages over vast distances? Do people communicate with magic mirrors? Seeing stones/Palantirs? Spells? In Dominic Ashen's *Steel and Thunder*, the characters communicate over long distances with magic—often with comical results.

3. How long do messages take to send and receive? Will people wait months for word from overseas, or is it available at the push of a button?

4. Is communication primarily verbal? Non-verbal? What type of communication is most prevalent among the people?

5. What about those who cannot speak/hear? Is sign language a thing?

6. Are there special methods of communication for certain situations (hand signals, secret vocabulary, passwords)? How do those situations apply to your plot and characters?

7. Can everyone read and write, or is this a special skill? How does the average person learn to read and write? Do they learn at home or go to school?

Part Three: But why did they do that

8. Is being a clerk a career? Do people seek others to write/read their messages for them?

9. How do people write in this world? Pen and paper or symbols carved into walls? How easy is it for people who live far apart to understand one another?

10. How rare are writing materials (paper, ink, papyrus, stone, etc.)? Is writing easily available, or does it require money for access?

11. Does the world have pencils (sturdy, use anywhere) or just pens (require quills, ink pots, sand, etc.)? That is: is writing portable? Does the average person have access to writing tools?

12. How are books distributed? Hand copies or movable type or scrolls xeroxed with magic? Print on demand or digital downloads? What's the new technology in your world?

___

13. Does the world have television to share news? Is the internet a thing?

___

14. How many languages are in the world? Who speaks what and why? Do people often know other languages? Does a lack of comprehension create conflict in your story?

___

15. Do different people use different dialects or accents in your world? Do these regional differences cause confusion? How does this affect your characters and plot?

___

Part Three: But why did they do that

16. How is communication monitored by those in power? Can the government spy on messages? Are messages regulated somehow? Are there things a person can't or shouldn't say?

17. How many other people would the average person be in communication with on a regular basis? Is it normal to have several pen pals or just to know the people in town?

18. Is propaganda a thing in your world? Do people believe things that are untrue because of how the information has been communicated?

19. Is there a group responsible for regulating communication? Can people make up new words or sounds (twerk, e-mail, etc.), or is that up to the discretion of a specialized group in the society?

20. How much does the average person know about communication techniques in the world?

_____
_____
_____

D1.
Earth-Variant Communication

1. What kinds of familiar communication practices do you use in your world? How do these forms of communication affect your plot?

2. What is the most common form of communication for your characters: cell phones, letters, in-person interactions? Why did you choose this method instead of another?

3. Non-verbal communication is critical in most interactions. What kinds of non-verbal signals do your characters share with one another? Does a head nod still mean yes while a head shake means no? What does a raised eyebrow convey?

The General Worldbuilding Guide

4. In what ways have you shifted modern communication methods for your story? Why did you make those changes?

5. How important is communication in your story? How much of your own communication style appears among the characters?

Part Three: But why did they do that 159

To: 24.

Subject: Communication Fun Activity:
I'm sorry, but I don't speak _____ .

Think about the people your characters will encounter. What languages do they speak? How will these differences affect the story?

Jot down a few words that may cause confusion for your characters—a homophone that sounds like an insult or something completely different from what it actually means.

Will your characters learn to speak other languages during their adventures or just a few words here and there? What are new words they may try out (and probably ruin the pronunciation in the process)?

Will your story include words you've created for unique things? List them and their usage here.

E. Technology

1. What level of technology exists in your world? Is it traditional with less modern tools: fire, irrigation, wheel, iron, gunpowder, windmill, compass or more progressive and modern: clock, printing, steam engine, railways, photography, telegraph, telephone, electricity, computer, internet?

___

2. How is technology powered—steam/coal/gas/electric/solar/magic/etc.? Is this a new invention, or has it been around for a while?

___

3. Who controls the technology? How does that group control it? Why? Are certain technologies forbidden or secret? Why?

___

4. How do people view advances in technology? Do they embrace changes eagerly or cling to older practices?

_____
_____
_____

5. Does the world have indoor plumbing? How does it work? Does everyone have it? Only the wealthy, or certain crafty folk?

_____
_____
_____

6. What are key inventions in your world? How much did these inventions affect the development of your world's civilizations?

_____
_____
_____

7. Do people track time? Are there watches, clocks, 8-hour candles?

_____
_____
_____

8. Is there electricity or electronic devices of any kind? How do they differ from the ones in our world?

_____
_____
_____

9. Has the internet been invented? How is it regulated, if at all? Does everyone have access? How do people use it (to post cat pictures, clearly)?

_____
_____
_____

10. Do people have cell phones? Video chat? How accessible is this technology to most people? Is this how people communicate in this world? How do people view those who can't or won't use this technology?

_____
_____
_____

11. How does technology interact with the natural forces in your world? In Lyra Saenz's *Prelude*, witches and technomancers fight with magic and technology.

_____
_____
_____

12. How has technology affected safety and self-defense? What devices are available for people to protect themselves from threats?

_____
_____
_____

13. Are there people in your world who refuse to use technology? Why? How are these groups viewed by others?

_____
_____
_____

14. Where did the technology in your world come from? Did the inhabitants of your world create it, or was it shared with them from another civilization?

_____
_____
_____

15. How much does the average person know about the available technology?

_____
_____
_____

E1.
Earth-Variant Technology

1. What technological abilities will feature in your story that are recognizable to your readers (cars, phones, internet, electricity, indoor plumbing, etc.)? Why did you choose to keep these elements of the real world?

___

2. What technological devices are unique to your world? Do they resemble items we have in the real world? What function do they perform that we do not have now (flying cars, teleportation, telepathy, etc.)? In Ty Carlson's *The Bench*, the bench allows users to reconnect with dead loved ones.

___

3. Are there certain technological abilities that you have specifically removed from your world (no phones, no cars, etc.)? Why did you remove those elements?

___

4. How important is technology to the story you are telling? Note the devices that play key roles in the plot.

_____
_____
_____

5. What is a device or invention that you imagine may exist in the near-future that you can include in your world as already invented? How can you use this technology in your story?

_____
_____
_____

GAME OVER

PLAY AGAIN?

YES NO

25

Technology Fun Activity:
Name That Device

What technology do your characters have handy? Why do they use it for?

Character Name	Available Tech	Use in Story

F. Travel

1. How much do people travel in your world? Can you drive 60 miles in an hour, or will it take several hours on horseback or a day and night of walking?

2. How often do people leave their homes or places of birth to see other parts of the world? Is it common to go to new places? Are travelers viewed with suspicion?

3. How do people view those who have never left home? Is this a mark of honor or of cowardice? What about those who travel extensively (think of the European Great Tour expected for most wealthy young men in the 1800s)? Is this something to be praised and coveted, or does it make the well-traveled stand out and seem foreign?

4. How far is considered "far away" in your world? Who would consider it to be "far away"? How relative is this concept? Does a person from a small town view "far away" as the big city in the distance? Or is "far away" on the other side of the globe?

___

5. What manner of travel is available, and how much does it cost? Can the average person afford to see faraway places?

___

6. Is there sea travel in your world? Boats, steamships, submarines? Is it common for people to cross the water, or is it expensive and dangerous? Are there established traveling routes between places?

___

7. Is there air travel in your world? Airplanes, hot air balloons, zeppelins, cyberwings? Are these modes of travel available for everyone or exclusively for certain groups?

___

8. How do people travel vast distances? Can they teleport via machine/magic? In TS Simons' series *Antipodes*, people in a post-apocalyptic world travel via portals to the opposite sides of the globe.

___

9. Where do people stay when they are traveling? Do they sleep under the stars, in a hotel, in a friendly farmer's barn, in a relative's living room? Do people welcome traveling strangers for the night as they are passing through? Are hotels a thing in your world? Inns? Airbnb?

___

10. Throughout history, different parts of the world have hosted jugglers, singers, acrobats, troubadours and the like as they traveled from place to place performing music or dance or plays or poetry. Is there an expectation for travelers to entertain guests in exchange for their meals and lodging? Is there a class of people like this in your world?

___

11. Is there an industry built up around travel? Are there guides and helpful world travelers willing to take people into unknown spaces? Are these guides known to be trustworthy, or will they lead you to the desert and abandon unsuspecting travelers?

12. How easy is it to move from house to house in your world? Do people pack up their belongings and live in a new place often? Do they move with boxes and U-Hauls or a blanket tied to a stick holding their worldly possessions? Is it normal for people to move from home to home?

___

13. What types of conveyances are available for travel? Is there a reliable train service, a bus route, Ubers, bicycles, a caravan, a man pulling a cart behind him? What is the most common way for people to move around the world?

___

14. Is travel a relatively simple thing (I get in my car and take a drive downtown), or is it a complicated endeavor (I pack the family into a covered wagon and head to Oregon)? How easy can people move from place to place?

___

15. How much does the average person know about travel?

F1. Earth-Variant Travel

1. What elements of travel from the real world feature in your world? Why did you keep these elements?

_____
_____
_____

2. How have you altered common methods of travel to suit your world or story? Why did you make these changes?

_____
_____
_____

3. Is the depiction of travel based on your own experiences, or are you imagining what it might be like to ride a train through the frozen countryside? How much research will you do to ensure that your travel strikes true for readers?

_____
_____
_____

4. We live in a modern world where travel is fairly easy in many places (though not always). But what happens when technology fails and your characters must resort to alternative methods? How can you use common travel issues (breakdowns, delays, lost baggage, detours due to natural disasters, etc.) in your world to enhance the realism?

_____

_____

_____

5. Many stories rely on the idea of travel for character growth. How important is travel to your story in this world?

_____

_____

_____

Part Three: But why did they do that

26.
Travel Fun Activity: Dream Vacation

Where do your characters dream of going for a vacation? Do they long for a sunny beach with palm trees or a cozy fireplace in the mountains or a long soak in a hot spring? If they could take off for a week, where would they go in your world? What would they do there?

Character	Where would they go for vacation?	Why would they go there?	What would they do there?	How can this affect the story you are telling?

G.
Health and Wellness (Medicine)

1. What is considered healthy in your world? How do people measure healthiness (BMI, physical appearance, age, number of stairs you can climb without getting out of breath)?

   _____
   _____
   _____

2. How does the world treat illness and disease? Has medical technology advanced enough to cure certain diseases? Doctor McCoy from *Star Trek* refers to dialysis as a barbaric practice and wonders why they don't just give patients the pill to cure diabetes.

   _____
   _____
   _____

3. What is a common medical treatment in this world? If a person breaks a leg, do they get roots and poultices or x-rays and crutches? Can medicine cure diabetes with a pill, or is it a death sentence?

___

4. What unique diseases/illnesses exist in your world that your characters will encounter? How does the cure/lack thereof affect the plotline? (Does Jack need to retrieve a talisman from another world because the doctors in his world can't cure cancer and save his mom like the Stephen King story?)

___

5. How do people view those who work with medicine or healing? Are doctors worshiped or under suspicion? Is medicine a secret knowledge known by masters and apprentices, or are there schools?

___

6. How does your world deal with mental health issues? Do they have effective methods for treatment, or do they just send people to asylums and hide them in attics? *Jane Eyre* features the classic "madwoman in the attic" who tries to kill everyone.

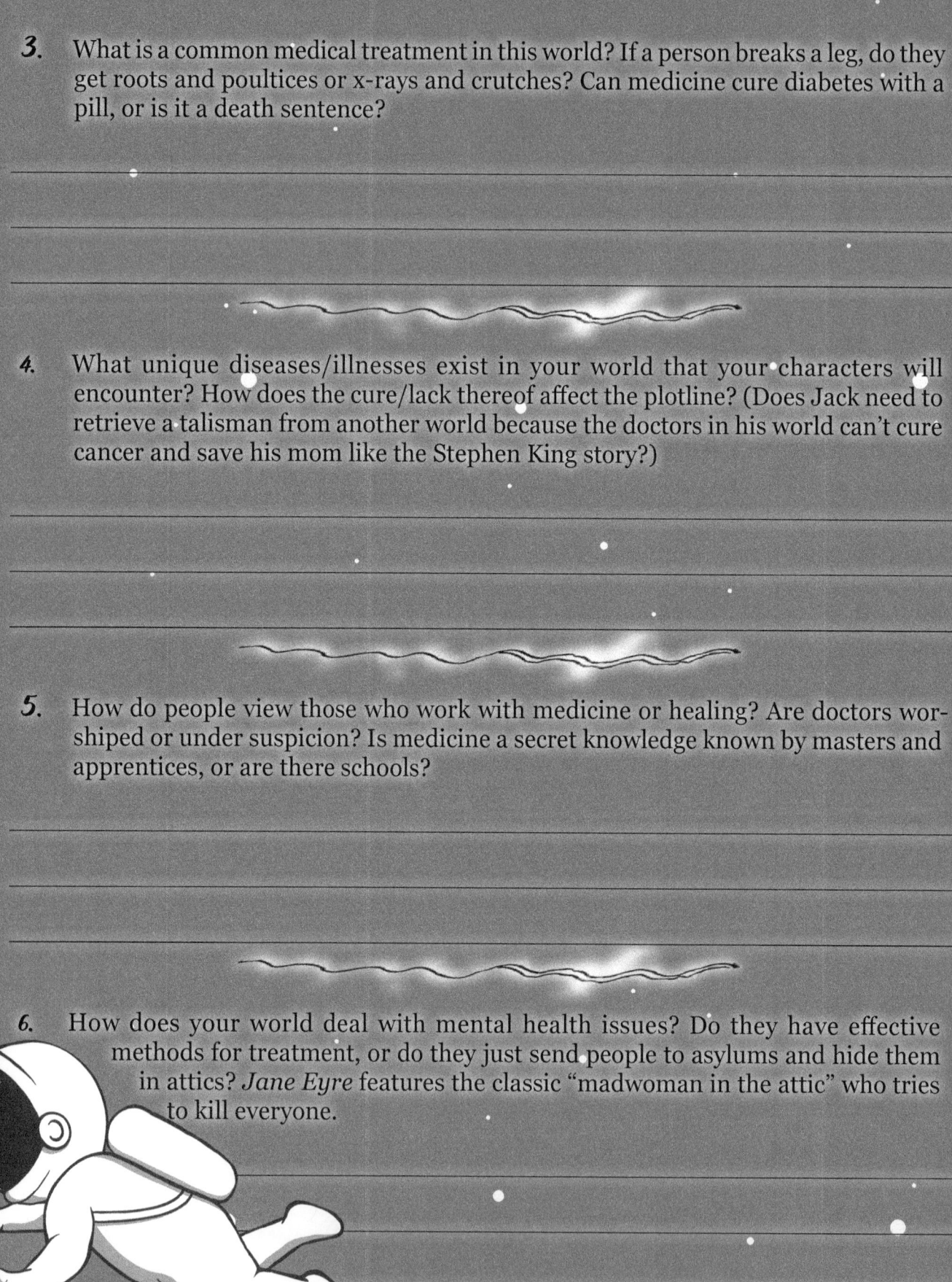

7. How does your world handle pregnancy and childbirth? Do women get modern medical care while pregnant, or is it up to nature until the baby is born? Are there midwives? Are pregnant people well cared for in hospitals, or is childbirth a possible death sentence due to lack of knowledge?

_____
_____
_____

8. How common is infant mortality? Do people have many children because so many sicken and die during childhood?

_____
_____
_____

9. Does your world have a way for women to get pregnant without traditional methods (IVF)? Is this a common practice or expensive or forbidden? Are babies still born the natural way as a result of sex, or are humans engineered somehow?

_____
_____
_____

10. What is the average life expectancy in your world? What are the common reasons for death in your world? Do people die of sickness or disease, or accidents and old age?

_____
_____

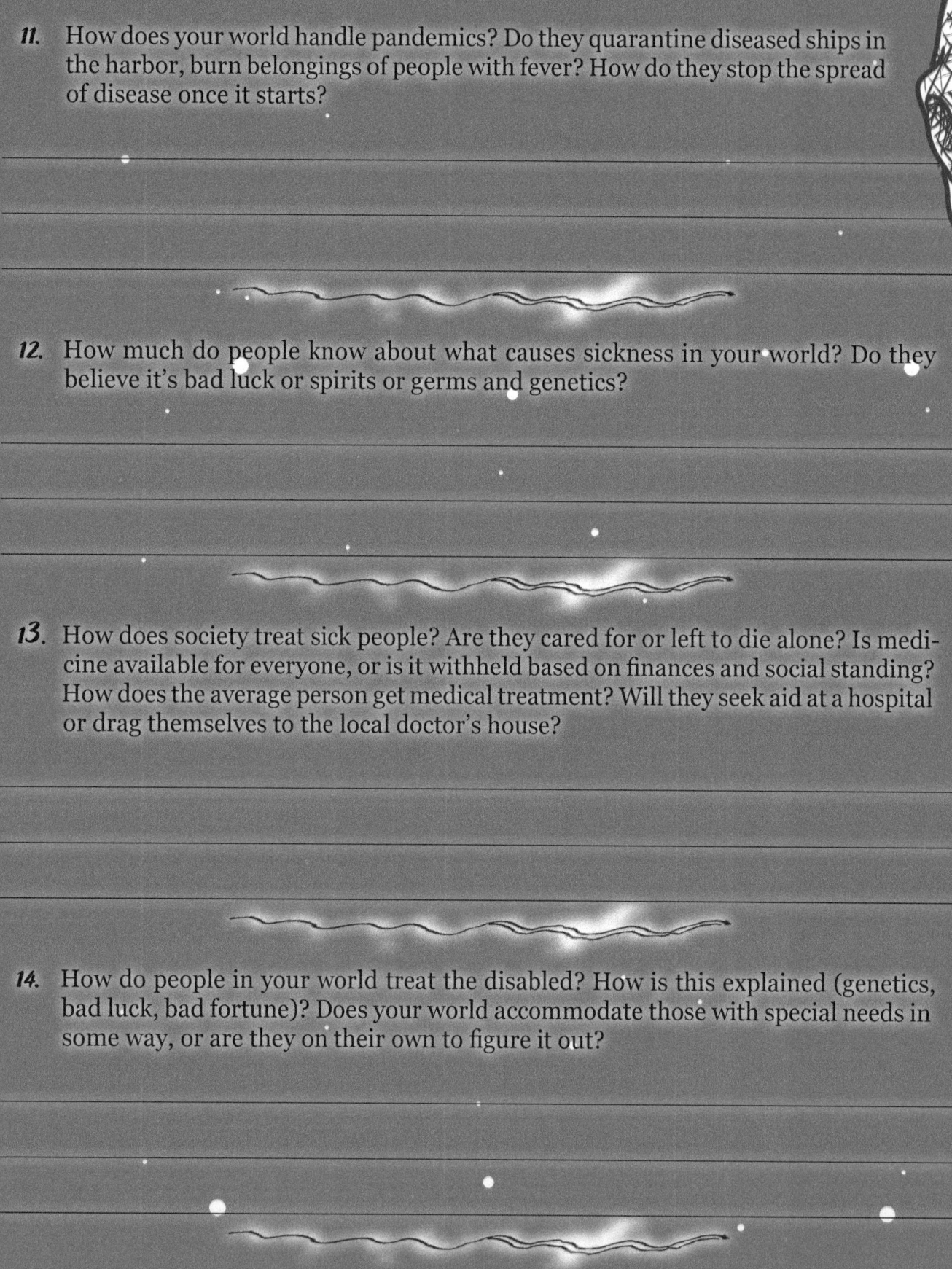

11. How does your world handle pandemics? Do they quarantine diseased ships in the harbor, burn belongings of people with fever? How do they stop the spread of disease once it starts?

_____
_____
_____

12. How much do people know about what causes sickness in your world? Do they believe it's bad luck or spirits or germs and genetics?

_____
_____
_____

13. How does society treat sick people? Are they cared for or left to die alone? Is medicine available for everyone, or is it withheld based on finances and social standing? How does the average person get medical treatment? Will they seek aid at a hospital or drag themselves to the local doctor's house?

_____
_____
_____

14. How do people in your world treat the disabled? How is this explained (genetics, bad luck, bad fortune)? Does your world accommodate those with special needs in some way, or are they on their own to figure it out?

_____
_____
_____

15. How healthy is the average person on the street in your world?

_____
_____
_____
_____

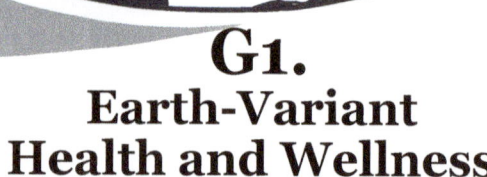

G1.
Earth-Variant Health and Wellness

1. Which elements of our world's healthcare system have you included in your world? Why those elements and not others?

   _____
   _____
   _____

2. How much of your experience with medicine and health care appears in your world? Do you need to research how certain illnesses are treated in order to portray them properly?

   _____
   _____
   _____

3. Do your characters get injured? How accurate is your depiction of medical treatment in terms of treating the injured human body?

   _____
   _____
   _____

4. Throughout history, humans have associated different diseases with moral judgment. Does that attitude appear in your world? Is a disease considered divine punishment?

_____
_____
_____

5. How many non-healthy people feature in your story? Do you show disabled people? Recovering people? Why did you focus on your characters and not others?

_____
_____
_____

27. Health and Wellness Fun Activity: Disease

What are some diseases that have affected the people in your world? Start with broad effects in the world at large and then drill down to specific effects on the characters.

Disease name	Causes (if known)	Signs/symptoms	Where does this appear in your story?	How does this affect your story?

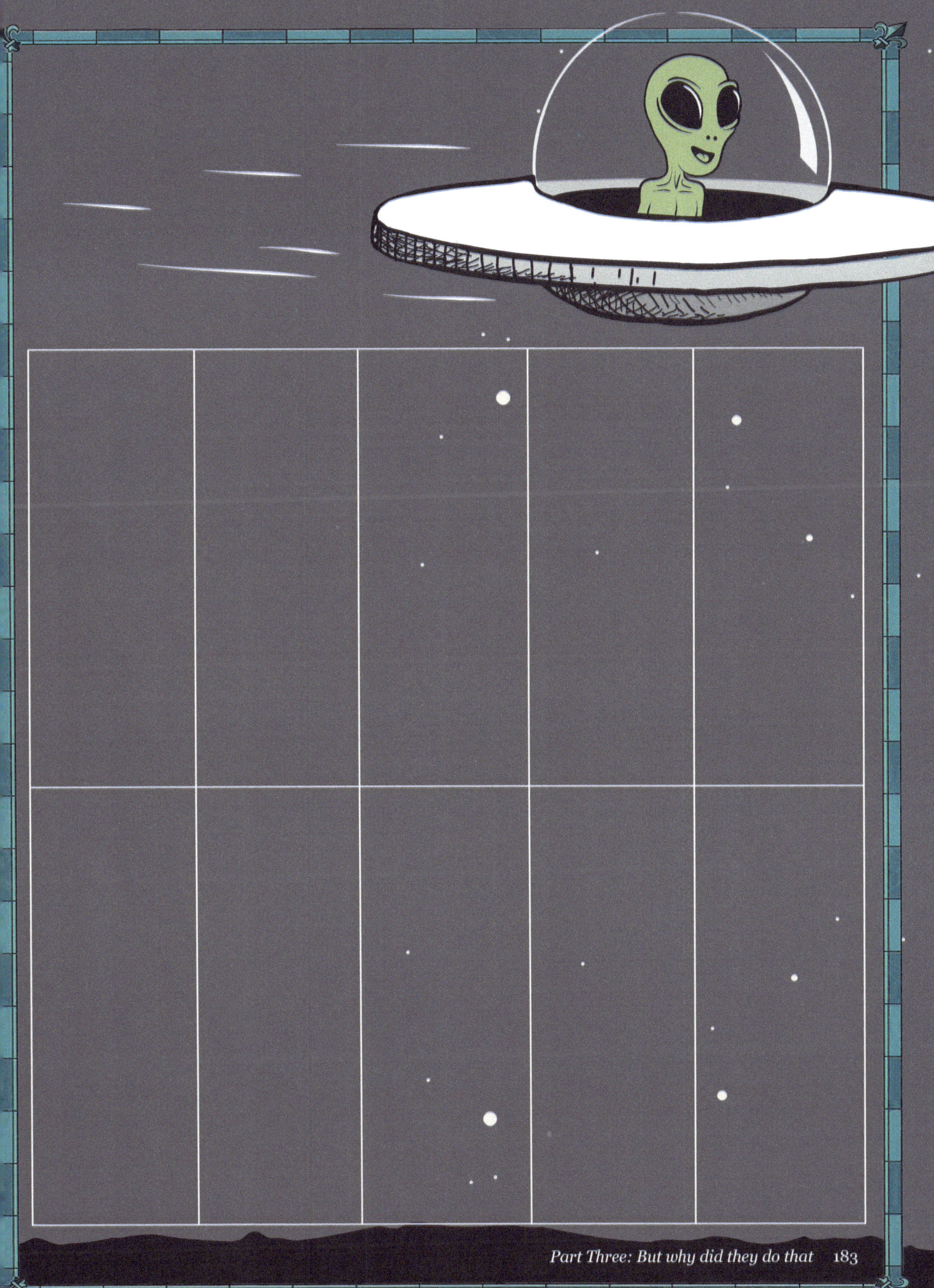

Build Your World Activities

28.
What is Truth?

Communication and technology are the building blocks on which you tell your story—the why and the how of it—but are these being abused in your world? What stories or "facts" do other people in your world believe that your characters have discovered are not true or have been modified in some way? Is this a point of tension in your story? How do these conflicting or false narratives affect your characters and the direction of your story? Which of your characters know what information? Below is a basic Johari Window used to enhance an individual's perception of others. Jot down some information for your characters to clarify the facts.

Character Name	Known to self	Not known to self
Known to others	What information does your character know that everyone else also knows?	What information do other people know that this character does not know?
Not known to others	What information does your character know that is not known to other people?	What information is unknown by both your character and everyone else (except the all-powerful author creator)?

	Known to self	Not known to self
Known to others		
Not known to others		

	Known to self	Not known to self
Known to others		
Not known to others		

	Known to self	Not known to self
Known to others		
Not known to others		

	Known to self	Not known to self
Known to others		
Not known to others		

Build Your World Activities

29. Motivation and Goals

What motivates your characters? How are these goals affected by your world's economy, educational paradigms, relationship standards, communication systems, technology, travel, and medicine? How do these forces push your story in a certain direction? How do these forces contribute to the conflicts in your story? Where do these concepts intersect?

	Motivation	Goal	Conflict
Economic factors			
Educational paradigms			
Relationship standards			

Communication systems			
Technology			
Travel			
Medicine			

30.
Your Story Time:
But why did they do that?

Now it's time to take notes on how this *information* will affect the story you have in mind. It's okay if the answer to some of these questions is "ABSOLUTELY NOTHING AT ALL!" Even if this information doesn't come into play directly, it's still good to have it in the back of your mind (in case an eager reader writes an email asking about it one day—you'll have a ready reply!).

1. You've considered your economic system and the effects on your world. How does this economy affect your story?

   _____
   _____
   _____
   _____

2. You've developed an educational system and how your characters interact with knowledge. How will these structures affect your story?

   _____
   _____
   _____
   _____

3. You've thought about how relationships work in your world. How will these expectations affect your story?

   _____
   _____
   _____
   _____

The General Worldbuilding Guide

4. You've established communication parameters for your world. How will these guidelines affect your story?

_____
_____
_____
_____

5. You've designed the technology level of your world. How will the availability of these conveniences affect your story? (Most of Buffy's problems would be solved by a cell phone!)

_____
_____
_____
_____

6. You've worked out how travel functions in your world. How will these methods affect your story?

_____
_____
_____
_____

7. You've described the treatment levels available to maintain health and wellness in your world. How will these medicines (or lack thereof) affect your story?

_____
_____
_____
_____

Build Your World Activities

USE THIS SPACE TO JOT DOWN ANY IDEAS THAT THIS EXERCISE HAS SPARKED—THEY MAY BE USEFUL AT SOME POINT!

Part Four: Mechanics

This section gets into the little details of your world—those things you don't think about until you're mid-sentence and need the word describing a specific thing in your world. This part starts with Science, moves into Nature and Weather, and ends with Measurements (time, distance, and weight).

A. Science

1. How do the laws of physics work in your world? Is it similar to our world, or are there unique features (time moves sideways)?

   _____
   _____
   _____

2. Is gravity stronger/weaker than earth? Can people "fall off" the world, or are they trapped by the force of gravity?

   _____
   _____
   _____

3. How does the environment affect the inhabitants? (Cold air can hurt your skin. Hot air makes you sweat.)

   _____
   _____
   _____

4. How can inhabitants affect the laws of physics? Can they move as fast as the speed of sound in machines like rocket jets? Can they slow a fall with large plastic wings (or a really big rubber raft)? Is this a special ability (inherent or learned), or can anyone do it?

_____
_____
_____

5. How does chemistry work in your world? What is different from our world? Are specific chemical reactions important to your story? (Lab accidents lead to zombies!)

_____
_____
_____

6. How does biology function in your world? How much do your inhabitants know about how bodies (of people or creatures) work?

_____
_____
_____

7. Is there a liquid/gas/solid division of matter or something else? How do your people quantify and label the physical world? What language do they use to name things as they are discovered (Latin or something else)?

_____
_____
_____

8. How does light behave in this world? Are there rainbows? What colors are visible? Can certain creatures see different colors?

___

9. Do certain creatures have the ability to experience scientific principles in a different way? Can your dragons "see" the wind or dogs "smell" colors?

___

10. Do these rules of science apply to your main character? Are there things that your character can do that other people can't (or can't without aid of some kind)?

___

11. Does your world explore a popular scientific theory (*Ender's Game*, *The Martian*, *Ready Player One*)?

___

12. How do your inhabitants study science? Is there an Academy? How do others view those who study science? Are they crazy scientists in lab coats or wild men in underground caves?

_____

_____

_____

13. Are people skeptical of science and scientific theories in your world? Do they trust more "natural" methods over seemingly "technological" methods for doing things? Why?

_____

_____

_____

14. Do people abuse science in this world? Are there major scientific corporations (Umbrella) working on new scientific/technological breakthroughs? How does that affect your characters and story?

_____

_____

_____

15. How much does the average person know about science?

_____

_____

_____

A1. Earth-Variant Science

1. How much of the science in your world is based on real scientific principles? Why these and not others?

   _____
   _____
   _____

2. Sometimes a great story takes a familiar concept and subtly shifts a "known" factor to create something new. What elements of science can you alter to change your world and impact your story?

   _____
   _____
   _____

3. Debates over scientific theory have fueled a number of historical conflicts (The earth is round, the sun is the center of the solar system, etc.). How does this relationship between science and history play into your world?

   _____
   _____
   _____

4. How well do you understand scientific principles? Do you need to research how things work in order to properly present them?

___

5. Many scientific principles are under attack in our world. Does your world disbelieve science when it doesn't suit the goal of those in power?

___

Part Four: Mechanics 199

31. Science Fun Activity

- List some of the unique scientific rules or principles that apply in your world.

- How do they work?
  _____
  _____
  _____
  _____

- How do these rules influence your story?
  _____
  _____
  _____
  _____

- How do these rules affect your characters?
  _____
  _____
  _____
  _____
  _____

B. Nature

1. What kind of flora and fauna does your world have? How does it differ from the real world?

    _____
    _____
    _____

2. Describe the natural environments that your characters may encounter: forests, deserts, islands, mountains, etc. How are they similar to ours? How are they different?

    _____
    _____
    _____

3. Do people use plants in medicine? How?

    _____
    _____
    _____

4. Is tea drinking a thing in your world? How did people figure out that they could steep certain plants and drink the tasty water?

_____
_____
_____

5. Are certain plants poisonous (or even venomous)? How did people figure out what was safe to use and how to use it? Did someone tell them, or was it trial and error? ("Bob died after eating that mushroom—I guess we shouldn't eat those.")

_____
_____
_____

6. How much technology and production is involved in the consumption of plant life in your world? Does everything get processed and sanitized, or do people pick it themselves?

_____
_____
_____

7. How does the natural world interact with the creatures and animals of your world?

_____
_____
_____

8. Does your world have special walking and talking plants, like Ents? How sentient is Nature in your world?

___

9. Where did the natural world come from? Was it created by a god, or is it a result of other natural phenomena (islands from ancient volcanic eruptions)?

___

10. How much does the average person know about Nature?

B1. Earth-Variant Nature

1. What familiar plants from this world will feature in your world? Why those and not others?

2. How much of our real-world attitudes toward Nature will be reflected in your world? What aspects will remain the same and which will shift? Why?

3. Will you spend a lot of time discussing Nature in your writing? How detailed do you need to be when building your world? Will characters spend a lot of time walking through forests with different kinds of trees?

4. How familiar are you with Nature, and how much will you need to research? Can you recall the shape of a palm frond, or do you need to google it? Do you need images of real world plants to use as models?

_____

_____

_____

5. Plants have other properties than existing and occasionally smelling lovely. How will you use those other aspects (medical uses, food applications, etc.) in your story?

_____

_____

_____

32.
Nature Fun Activity: Name that plant!

Think about the plants your characters will encounter that are specific to your world. Describe the plants that fill the background of your story.

Name of Plant				
Location				
Common/Rare				
Physical Description				
Uses				
Special Properties				
How does your character encounter this plant?				

The General Worldbuilding Guide

C. Weather

1. What is the typical weather in your world? Are there seasonal changes? Describe these shifts.

   _____
   _____
   _____

2. Is your world big enough to have different seasons at the same time (winter in North and summer in South)?

   _____
   _____
   _____

3. What are some typical weather patterns in your world? Is it the stuff we know: snowstorms, rain, humidity, sunshine, and clouds?

   _____
   _____
   _____

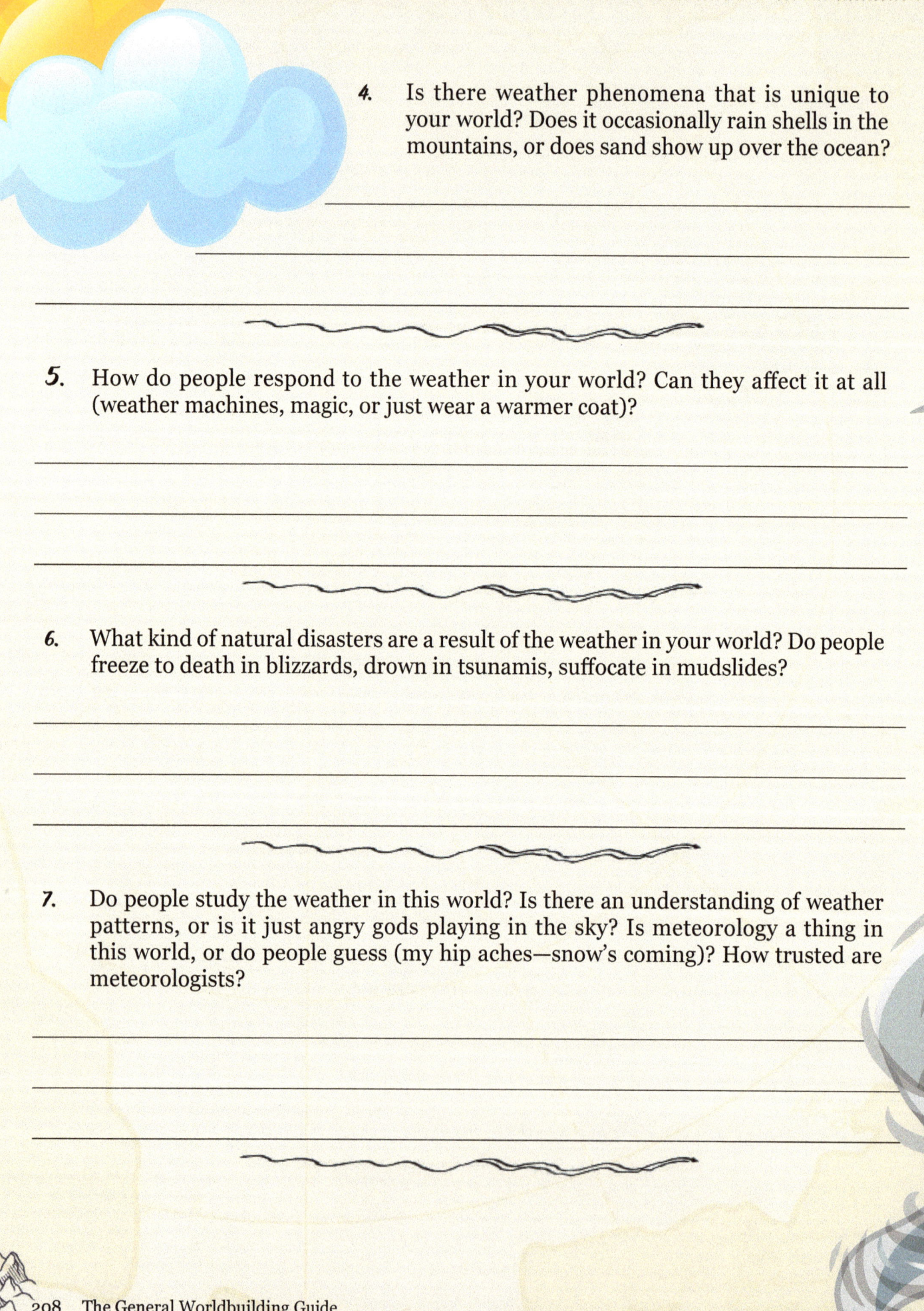

4. Is there weather phenomena that is unique to your world? Does it occasionally rain shells in the mountains, or does sand show up over the ocean?

___

5. How do people respond to the weather in your world? Can they affect it at all (weather machines, magic, or just wear a warmer coat)?

___

6. What kind of natural disasters are a result of the weather in your world? Do people freeze to death in blizzards, drown in tsunamis, suffocate in mudslides?

___

7. Do people study the weather in this world? Is there an understanding of weather patterns, or is it just angry gods playing in the sky? Is meteorology a thing in this world, or do people guess (my hip aches—snow's coming)? How trusted are meteorologists?

___

8. Is the weather changing, or has it always been this way? Are the inhabitants of the world affecting the weather patterns (climate change)?

___

9. Do people have special names for different seasons in your world? What are they?

___

10. How much does the average person know about the weather in your world?

C1. Earth-Variant Weather

1. What weather events from our world will you incorporate in your world? Why those and not others?

   _____
   _____
   _____

2. Describing the weather in our world is easy enough based on the location of the situation: it's colder in the North and warmer in the South. Does your world have such distinctions?

   _____
   _____
   _____

3. In our world, science explains natural phenomena (thunderstorms, hurricanes, blizzards, etc.). How do the inhabitants of your world explain why natural events happen?

   _____
   _____
   _____

4. In our world, we are often at the mercy of the weather. How much agency do the inhabitants of your world have when it comes to the weather? Can they make it rain?

5. How much personal experience do you have with certain weather phenomena, and what will you have to research?

33. Weather Fun Activity

Create a weather tracker for your world (or at least one location in your world—pick the dominant one in your story)! What are the seasons of the year? What is the weather like during those seasons?

Season 1	
Season 2	
Season 3	
Season 4	

D. Measuring Time, Distance, and Weight

1. How does time work? Do people keep track of the passage of time closely, in hours and minutes and seconds, or more generally, like fall and spring?

2. How long is a day? How long is a night? Why are days and nights that long—is it the rotation of the planet, or are there magic tree lamps that wax and wane? Is time measured by light/dark periods? Or do people measure with a different metric—hours of rest or a set period that follows some other system?

3. Who determines the calendar? Think about years, months, weeks, days, hours, minutes, and seconds (and nanoseconds and beyond!). How does your world use these units of measurement?

4. What is considered "a long time" in your world?

_____
_____
_____
_____

5. What is the system of measurement used for distance in this world? Is it measured by miles, kilometers, meters, yards, feet, inches, centimeters or by the amount of time it takes to get somewhere (like old school latitude and longitude—six days, five hours, twelve minutes, and six seconds)?

_____
_____
_____
_____

6. Do people use common items for measurement (hands for horses), or are there official tools like rulers and protractors to keep things consistent? Does everyone use the same system, or do different systems cause confusion between groups? What is considered "far away" in your world?

_____
_____
_____
_____

7. How do people describe weight in this world? Do they follow a pounds/kilograms system, or do they use something else (stone)? Is something two dogs heavy or five feathers light?

_____
_____
_____
_____

8. How much can the average person carry? How much can they push? Pull? Drag?

___

9. Is there an institute or academy responsible for official weights and measures, or do people estimate such things?

___

10. How much does the average person know about the passage of time, measuring distance, and establishing weight?

34. Measurements Fun Activity: Vocabulary Time

What are some of the measurements you will use in your story? What words will your characters use to convey this information?

- How do characters describe time? What words do they use to measure the passage of time?

_____
_____
_____
_____

- What words do people use to describe distances?

_____
_____
_____
_____

- How do people explain the weight of an item? What terms are commonly understood?

_____
_____
_____
_____

35.
Measurement Fun Activity: Calendar Time

Create a calendar for your world (or at least one culture in your world—pick the dominant one in your story)! How do your seasons divide into months and weeks and days?

Seasons	
Months	
Weeks	
Days	

Part Four: Mechanics

Build Your World Activities

36.
It's Science!

Much of what people consider mystical in the world can be explained by scientific principles. How do your characters feel about this? Do they believe in a world beyond that which can be observed and recorded?

Character				
Science can explain...				
Science tries to explain ... but I'm not buying it				
Science cannot explain this...				

37. It's perfectly natural

Many stories have characters roaming the wilds at some point. What kinds of specific plant life will your characters encounter that will be significant to the story? Does a tree fall on someone, setting events into motion? Does a misplaced bouquet lead to awkward expectations or romantic feelings? Even a couple falling in love in the city will see a flower here and there (or a seedling cracking the sidewalk). Do any plants have a special significance for your story? Stephen King wrote seven novels about a rose in a vacant lot. Surely, you have one plant that means something!

Build Your World Activities

38. Like the weather

Writers like to use the weather to reflect the mood of a scene. What desperate kiss isn't enhanced by the pouring rain? While readers may know that the reality of standing in a downpour may not match the fantasy, they will expect weather phenomena in your story, even if it's not a huge plot point. What are some moments where you can adjust the weather to affect the story you are telling? In *Klauden's Ring*, Hannah and Rory grow closer after being forced to hide from an epic storm in a cave.

39. Measure me!

It's easy to get derailed while writing when you need to figure out a measurement. Take a moment to work out the comparable terms in your world for common measurements in ours.

	Real world	Your world
Time		
Distance		
Weight		

40. Your Story Time: Mechanics

Now it's time to take notes on how this *information* will affect the story you have in mind. It's okay if the answer to some of these questions is "ABSOLUTELY NOTHING AT ALL!" Even if this information doesn't come into play directly, it's still good to have it in the back of your mind (in case an eager reader writes an email asking about it one day—you'll have a ready reply!).

1. You've considered how science operates in your world. How do these details show up in your story?

   _____
   _____
   _____
   _____

2. You've analyzed the natural world by describing the flora and fauna of your world. How will these plants appear in your story?

   _____
   _____
   _____
   _____

3. You've thought about the weather common in your world. How will the weather affect your story?

   _____
   _____
   _____
   _____

4. You've established terminology for measuring time, distance, and weight. When will these terms come into play in your story?

_____
_____
_____
_____

Build Your World Activities   225

USE THIS SPACE TO JOT DOWN ANY OTHER IDEAS THAT THIS EXERCISE HAS SPARKED—THEY MAY BE USEFUL AT SOME POINT!

Part Five:
Who lives in your world?

This section focuses on the inhabitants of your world: People and Creatures. These questions are open-ended and will work for any world. If you'd like a more genre-specific approach, check out the *Fantasy* and *Science Fiction* versions of this book for expanded questions.

A. People

1. What are the main groups of people in your world? If you have more than human, spend time developing each group's physical attributes, mental capabilities, and cultural quirks.

   _____
   _____
   _____

2. What are the cultural biases of each group? Do the Northerners judge the Southerners because they spend too much time in the sun? Do the East Coasters think the Islanders eat weird food? How does each group feel about those nearby? What about those who live far away?

   _____
   _____
   _____

3. Where do the cultural biases come from? Are they adapted from other group ideologies? Is there a specific event (war, famine, ruler, natural catastrophe) that led to these attitudes about other people?

   _____
   _____
   _____

4. Is the culture of certain groups similar? Why? Is it because they developed geographically close to one another, or is there another reason for the resemblance?

___

5. What groups have very different cultures? Why? Are they just far apart, or are there other factors that contribute to the way they live (geographic, catastrophic, agricultural, environmental)?

___

6. Have the cultures always been this way? Have there been major changes? If so, why did they change? Was there a terrible drought followed by an awful volcanic eruption, or ongoing warfare and an epic asteroid?

___

Part Five: Who lives in your world

7. What do the different groups believe—about themselves/about one another? Track the belief systems in some way. This will start to get fuzzy around book three, and unless you want to re-read your entire series every time you start a new novel, keep track of this information somewhere.

_____
_____
_____

8. What are the physical attributes of each group? If they are physically different, what do they look like? Are the people along the coastline built to hold their breath for diving deep below the waves? Are the people in the high tundra super pale to survive the cold?

_____
_____
_____

9. What are the mental attributes of each group? Are certain groups known for their wit, their stubborn streak, their loyalty? Do certain groups possess specific characteristics? Are city dwellers somehow charming or jungle folk super graceful?

_____
_____
_____

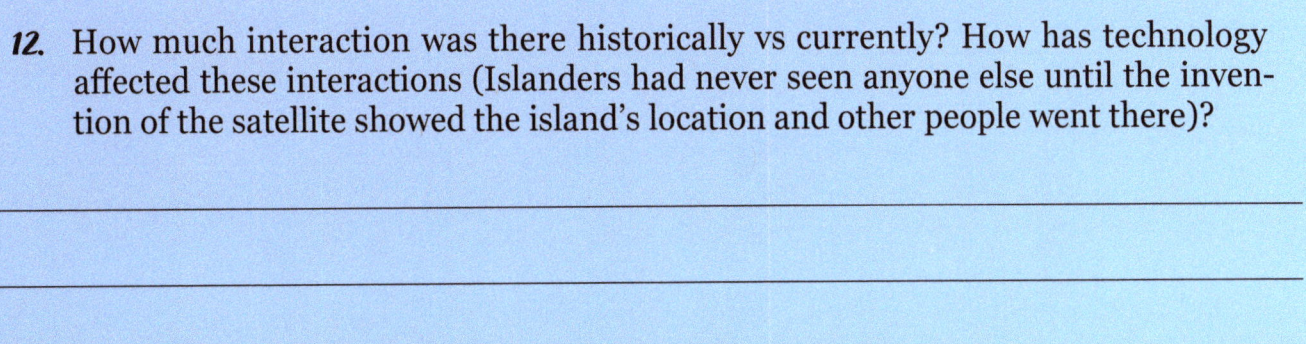

10. How do the groups interact in your world? Is there a history of cooperation between Southerners and Islanders but friction between Islanders and Hillfolk? Why? What happened to start this relationship?

_____
_____
_____

11. How much do certain groups interact? Do the Northerners see the odd Islander who has ventured across the ocean to the mainland, or is this a regular melting pot of people and cultures?

_____
_____
_____

12. How much interaction was there historically vs currently? How has technology affected these interactions (Islanders had never seen anyone else until the invention of the satellite showed the island's location and other people went there)?

_____
_____
_____

Part Five: Who lives in your world

13. How do groups view relationships between different species/races/groups? Is it accepted for people to marry/cohabitate with strangers/ travelers? Is it encouraged by some people?

_____

_____

_____

14. Out of all the people, which group is oldest? Which group existed first (or who says they did)? How do the people know their history is true? Is there a reliable written history that people can see? Are there immortal beings who were there at the start ("I was there, Gandalf…")? How much does the average person know about the history of their people? Are the groups' histories easily accessible to members? Are these histories accurate? Why or why not?

_____

_____

_____

15. How much does the average person know about other groups of people (species/races/ locations)?

_____

_____

_____

_____

A1.
Earth-Variant People

1. How do the groups of people in your world compare to the recognizable ones in our world? Why did you choose to include these people in your world and story?

___
___
___

2. How much has history influenced your portrayal of how well (or not) different groups get along? Do you have a version of Israel/Palestine in the Middle East? A Russia/Ukraine conflict?

___
___
___

3. How much of your personal experience with different groups in our world has made it into your world? Why did you keep those details and not others? In *Witch of the Black Circle*, Maria DeVivo carefully reconstructs the "Satanic Panic" fear of the 1980's to create a compelling story that walks the edge between truth and fiction.

___
___
___

4. How much research do you need to do to avoid stereotyping? How can you ensure you are portraying different groups of people accurately?

_____
_____
_____

5. How important is the relationship between different groups of people in your own story? Will conflicts or alliances be key elements or just background material?

_____
_____
_____
_____

41.
People Fun Activity: The World at a Glance

It's time to stereotype! Yes, every person is a unique individual, but when you are creating a background for your world, it helps to paint in broad strokes from time to time. Think about a few groups of people in your world and how they are perceived.

People/ Group Name				
Physical Description				
Mental Attributes				

Part Five: Who lives in your world

Special Skills/Abilities				
Geographic Location/Details				
Religious Beliefs				
Technology Level				

Food Habits				
Unique Cultural Practices				
How do these people fit into your story?				

42.
Fight Club

Time for the tough questions. Think about the different people who inhabit your world.

1. Out of all the people, who would win a physical fight? Which species is strongest? How/why would they win?

   _____
   _____
   _____
   _____

2. Out of all the people, who would win a mental fight—a battle of wits? Who is smartest? How/why would they win?

   _____
   _____
   _____
   _____

3. Out of all the people, who would win a fight using technology (or magic)? Whose toys are superior? How/why would they win?

   _____
   _____
   _____
   _____

43. Traditional or Progressive? Fun Activity

Think about where each group of people falls in terms of a more traditional (hunter/gatherer) or more progressive (technology/machines) society. Use the chart below to graph different groups in relation to one another.

Traditional	Mixture of Both	Progressive

B. Creatures

1. What kind of creatures live in your world? What animals will your characters encounter during the story?

_____
_____
_____

2. Are there recognizable animals—horses, deer, mice? Do they behave in expected ways, or do they have quirks unique to your world?

_____
_____
_____

3. Which animals/creatures are considered "friendly" or qualify to be a pet to the people in your world? Why?

_____
_____
_____
_____

4. What animals/creatures are considered food sources? Why this categorization for what is acceptable to consume?

___

5. Are animals/creatures raised as livestock? Which ones and where? How much of an industry is this, and how does it affect your story?

___

6. Do people raise animals/creatures for non-consumption? How is this practice viewed by the different inhabitants of your world? What creatures fill a farm in your world?

___

7. What is the dominant genus in your world at the moment? Right now, we're in the age of mammals—but is your world in the age of reptiles or insects?

___

Part Five: Who lives in your world

8. Are there mythological creatures—unicorns, basilisks, phoenixes? Do they follow traditional patterns, or do they have a special spin in your world?

_____

_____

_____

9. Where do the different animals/creatures live? How will your characters encounter them (stories, attacks, warnings, inspirations, etc.)?

_____

_____

_____

10. How familiar is the average person with certain animals/creatures? Are there animal/creature specialists in this world? If your characters want to learn about whales, where do they need to go—library, fish market, grizzled sea captain, marine biologist in town?

_____

_____

_____

11. Are there veterinarians in your world? What animals do they normally work on/with? What would be a strange creature for a vet to treat?

_____

_____

_____

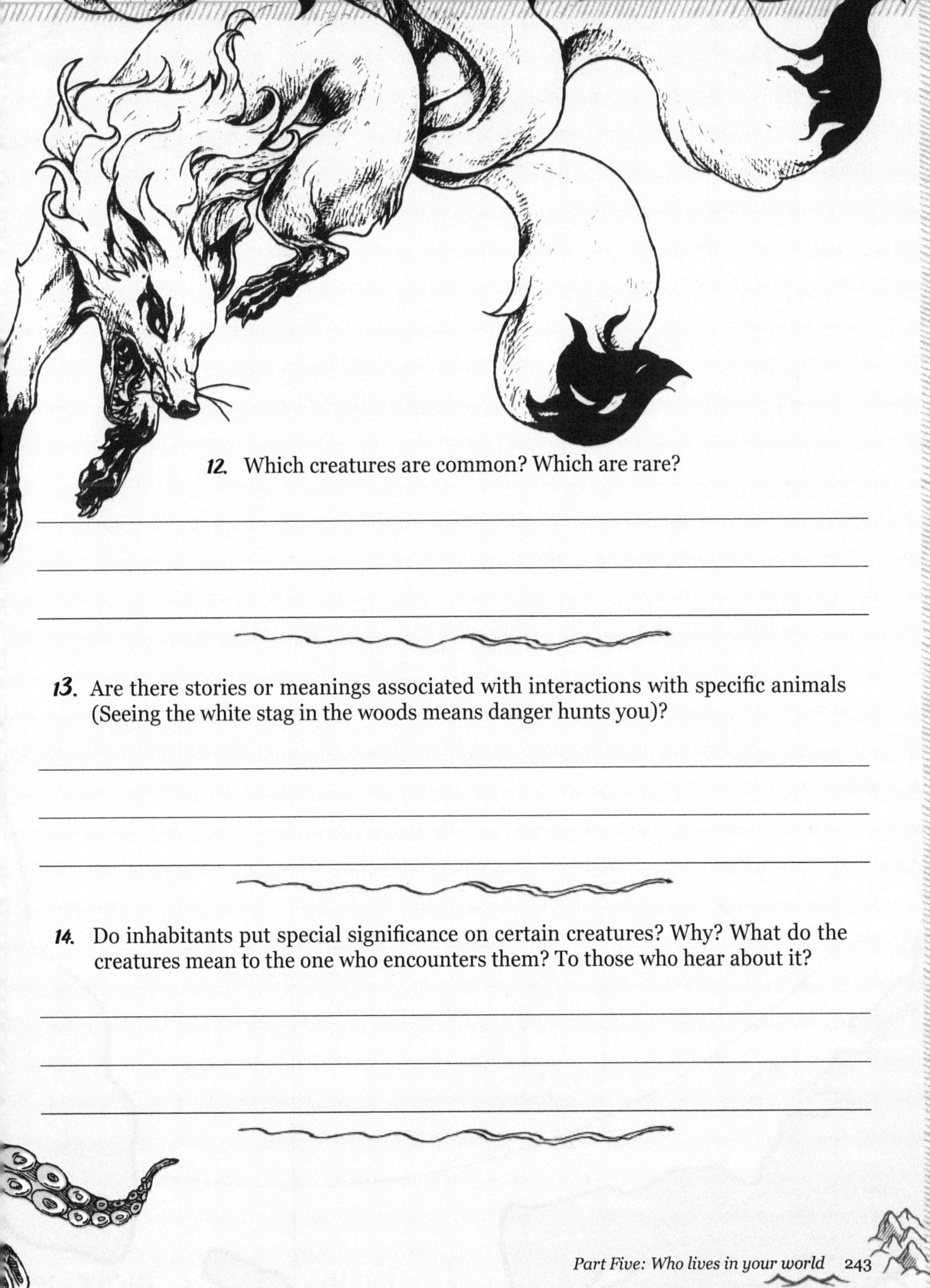

12. Which creatures are common? Which are rare?

13. Are there stories or meanings associated with interactions with specific animals (Seeing the white stag in the woods means danger hunts you)?

14. Do inhabitants put special significance on certain creatures? Why? What do the creatures mean to the one who encounters them? To those who hear about it?

15. Do animals/creatures talk in your world? What do they say? How do they communicate? Is it just literal speech, or is there an elaborate set of circumstances (If you ingest dragon blood, you can comprehend the language of birds like Sigurd)?

_____

_____

_____

16. If creatures can't speak the normal languages, can inhabitants communicate with them in other ways? Is this common or a rare ability (Parseltongue)?

_____

_____

_____

17. Do inhabitants hunt certain creatures? How do people feel about this practice? Have certain creatures been hunted to extinction? Is hunting regulated at all? In what way?

_____

_____

_____

18. Is there a hierarchy in the way people view creatures in your world? Eagles are awesome but pigeons are just meh?

_____

_____

_____

19. What is the typical relationship between people and creatures in this world? Are there animal familiars? Animal companions? Pets?

_____
_____
_____

20. How much does the average person in this world know about different creatures?

_____
_____
_____

Part Five: Who lives in your world

B1. Earth-Variant Creatures

1. What familiar creatures inhabit your world? Why keep these and not others?

   _____
   _____
   _____

2. How much experience do you have with the earth-version of these creatures: zoo, internet, farm, "I have one"? How much research will you put into your depiction of animals?

   _____
   _____
   _____

3. Horses are a common animal in fiction, but sometimes authors write about them without having any idea how horses actually behave (or what they require in order to stay healthy). How much do you actually know about horses? Do you need to do more research?

   _____
   _____
   _____

4. Will your inhabitants have pets? Why or why not? What kinds of creatures qualify as pets?

_____

_____

_____

_____

_____

5. Will you have common creatures (dogs, birds, elephants) behaving in different ways in your story? What will they do that they don't do in real life?

_____

_____

_____

_____

44. Creature Fun Activity

Time to take stock. Fill out the rankings below! List all of your creatures until you find the strongest.

- Which creature would win in a physical fight/war?

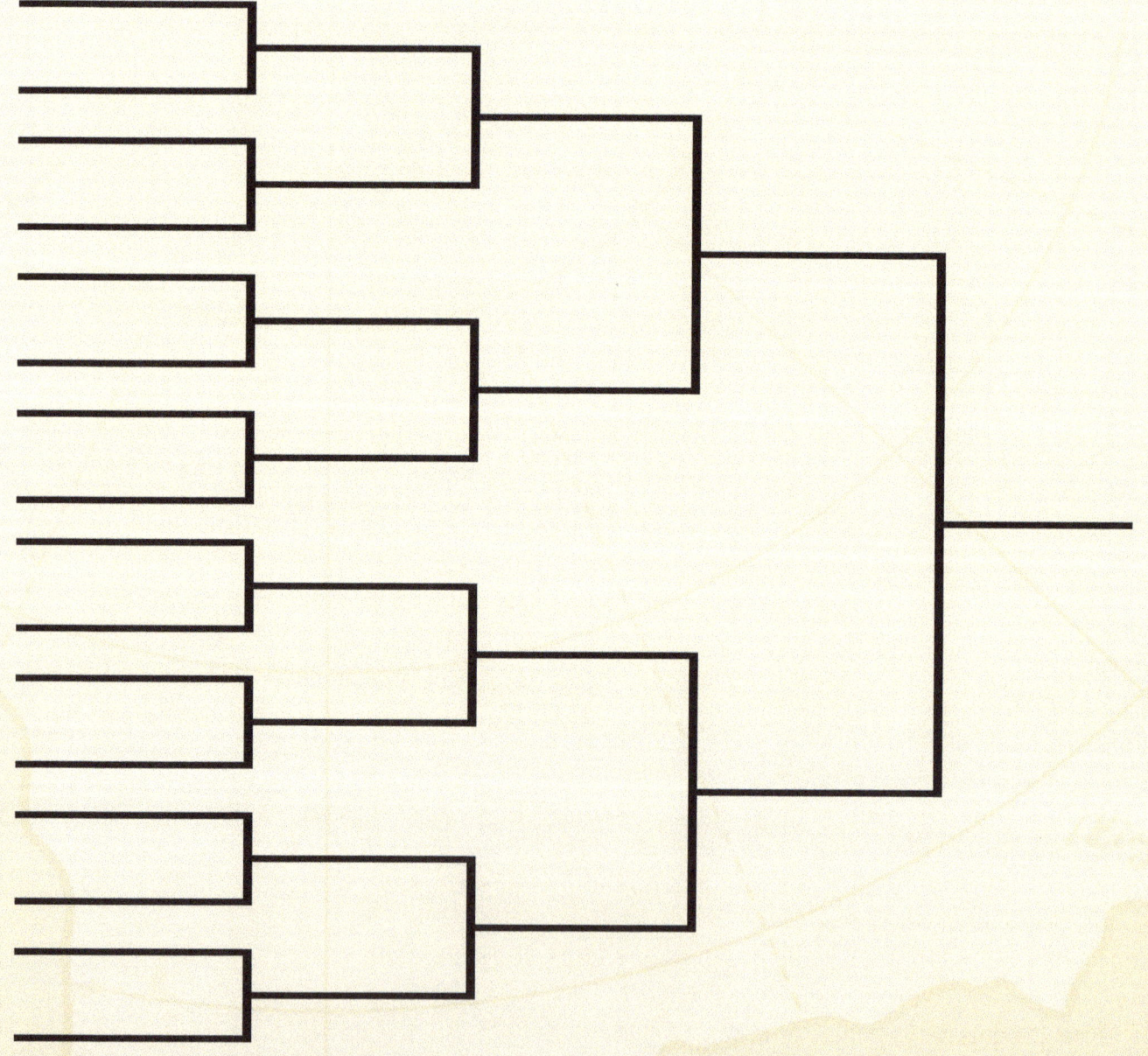

- Which creature would win during a mental/emotional fight?

45. I once had a...

What animal companions have your characters had in their lives? Did your main character own a goldfish or a ferret or a horse? Time to list the pet/animal companion history of your cast of characters.

Character				
Pets				
Animal Companion				
Creature				
Other				

Build Your World Activities

46.
Ancestry Time

Where did your characters come from? Who are their parents, grandparents, and on back through the generations? Take some time to work out a family tree for each of your main characters. For instance, in *Klauden's Ring*, I needed to know how every character was related, so I went back *four generations* to visualize those connections.

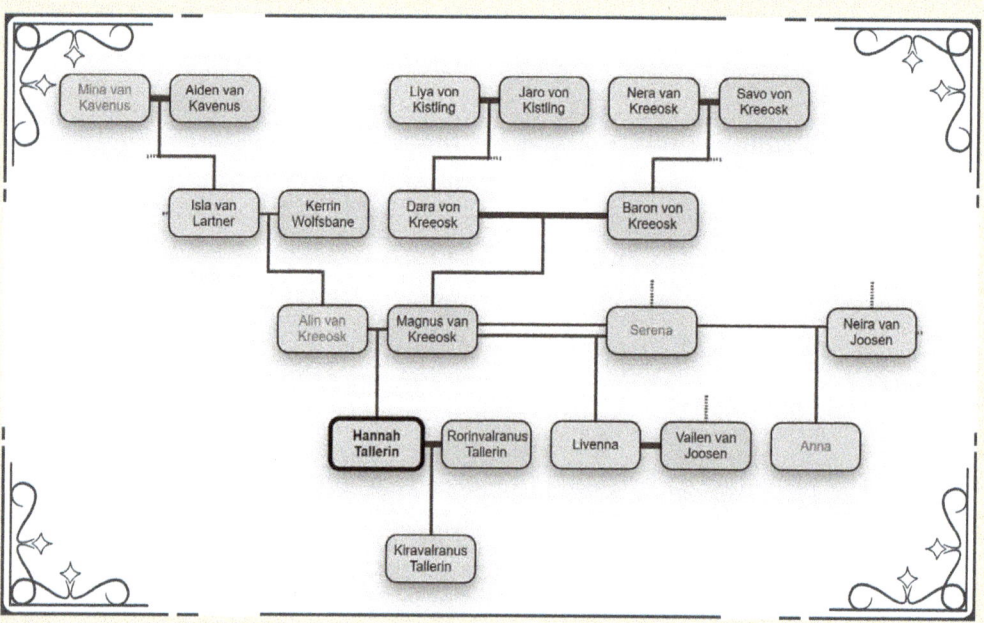

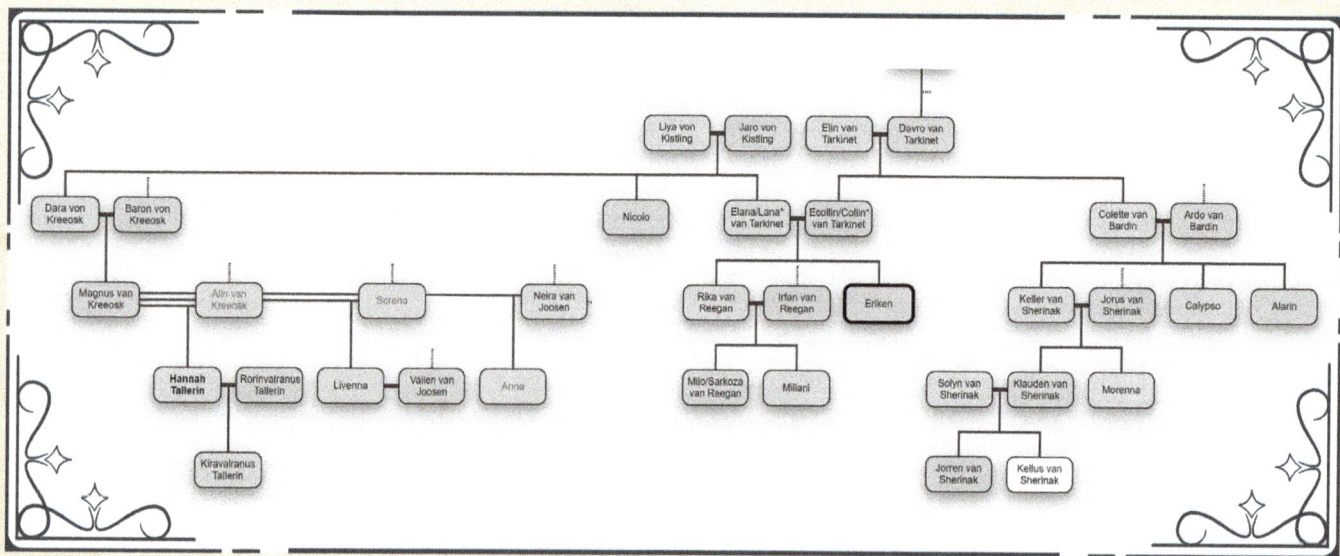

If you want to see more of Hannah's heritage, check out The InBetween by JM Paquette!

Build Your World Activities 253

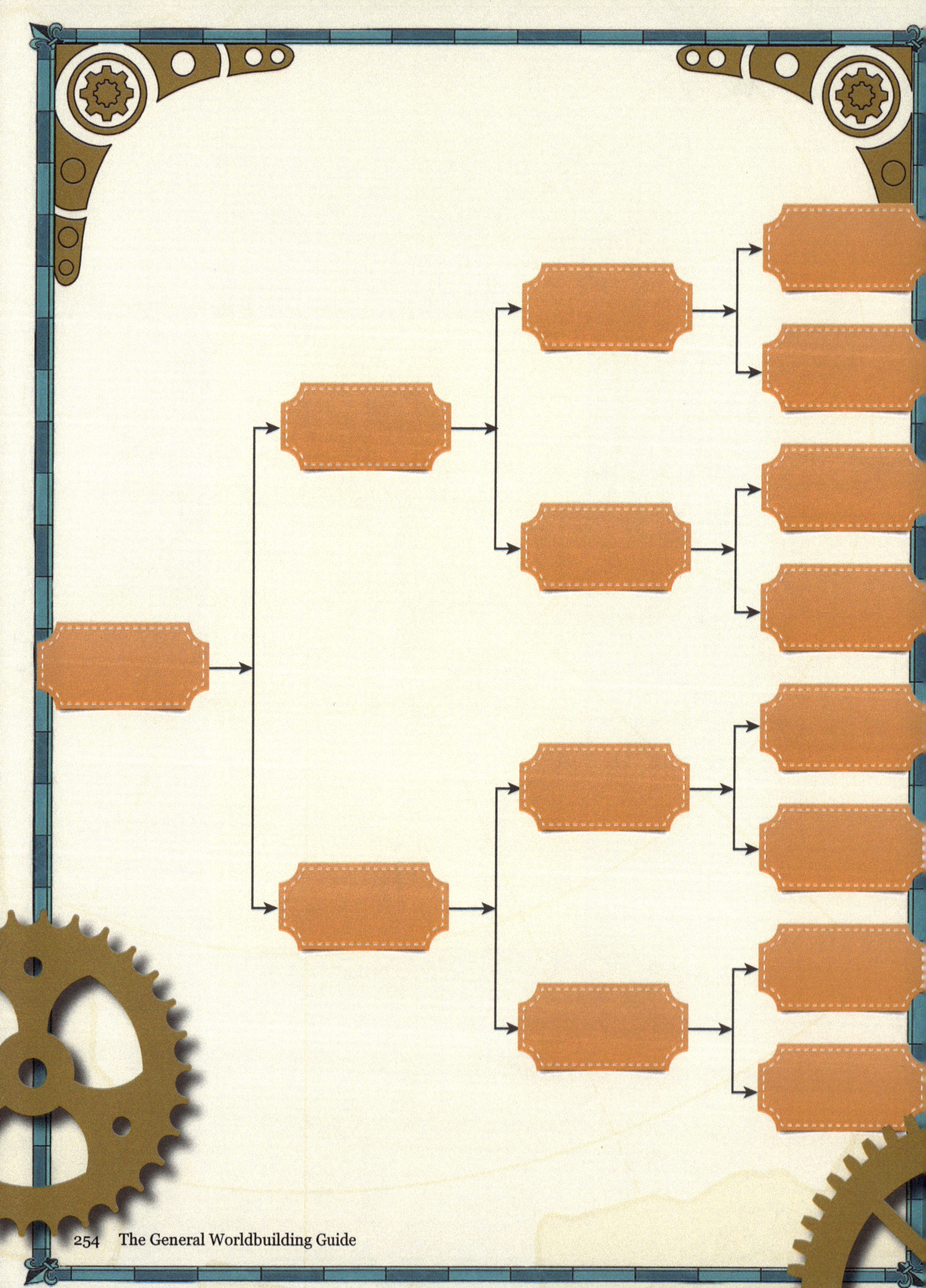

BUILD YOUR OWN FAMILY TREE IN THE SPACE BELOW!

47. When did that start?

My characters are constantly nodding and shrugging. To avoid falling into this trap, I make a list of OTHER movements that my characters do to display their emotions. In *Klauden's Ring*, Rory rotates his shoulder to show he's ready for a fight, or grins, showing his teeth, when he's in a good mood. Rory also has a chipped tooth and a shoulder filled with scars (morning star encounter). What tics or movements do your character use to show *internal conflict*? What physical marks or scars do your characters have? Characters with unique behaviors are exciting to write (and read!) about. The soul-servant Billy in *Invite Me In* has a tendency to wreck libraries because he sorts books by title (forming haikus to reflect his inner turmoil). What specific actions or behaviors do your characters have? How and why did these behaviors begin?

Character			
Physical scars/Marks			
Tics/Movements			
Behaviors			

48.
Eagles over Pigeons, hands down.

Now it's time to rank your creatures based on how people view them. What animals are considered "the best" in their category?

	Flying	Swimming	Land-based	Cuteness	Intelligence
Absolute Best					
Pretty Awesome					
Perfectly Adequate					
Serviceable					
No, thanks.					

Build Your World Activities

49.
How to hunt a bear ... in winter

In the Beowulf retelling *The 13th Warrior*, the men believe they are hunting bears responsible for *heinous violence*. They adjust their tactics once they realize what creature they seek, knowing that in the winter, they will find bears in caves. Even if your characters aren't hunting a creature, they may find themselves seeking something specific in your story. What is the general consensus in your world about successfully locating that particular creature (or **THING**)?

50. Your Story Time: Who lives in your world?

Now it's time to take notes on how this *information* will affect the story you have in mind. It's okay if the answer to some of these questions is "ABSOLUTELY NOTHING AT ALL!" Even if this information doesn't come into play directly, it's still good to have it in the back of your mind (in case an eager reader writes an email asking about it one day—you'll have a ready reply!).

1. You've considered who lives in your world. How do these groups of people affect your story?

   _____
   _____
   _____
   _____

2. You've decided which creatures inhabit your world. How will these animals interact with your storyline?

   _____
   _____
   _____
   _____
   _____

Build Your World Activities

USE THIS SPACE TO JOT DOWN ANY IDEAS THIS EXERCISE HAS SPARKED—THEY MAY BE USEFUL AT SOME POINT!

Part Six: Useful Stuff

A. Character Card:
Describe your characters all in one place!

USE THIS SPACE TO JOT DOWN ANY NOTES.

Name: _____
_____
Age: _____
Birthday: _____
Species/Race: _____
_____
Culture: _____
_____
_____
_____

Physical Description: _____
_____
Family Tree: _____
_____
Background: _____
_____
Weapon: _____
Place of Origin: _____
Known Locations: _____
Companions: _____
Aliases: _____
Associations: _____
Important Life Events: _____
_____

Name: _____

Age: _____

Birthday: _____

Species/Race: _____

Culture: _____
_____
_____

Physical Description: _____
_____

Family Tree: _____
_____

Background: _____
_____
_____

Weapon: _____

Place of Origin: _____

Known Locations: _____

Companions: _____

Aliases: _____

Associations: _____

Important Life Events: _____
_____

Name: _____
_____

Age: _____

Birthday: _____

Species/Race: _____
_____

Culture: _____
_____
_____

Physical Description: _____
_____

Family Tree: _____
_____

Background: _____
_____

Weapon: _____

Place of Origin: _____

Known Locations: _____

Companions: _____

Aliases: _____

Associations: _____

Important Life Events: _____
_____

Name: _____
_____

Age: _____

Birthday: _____

Species/Race: _____
_____

Culture: _____
_____
_____
_____

Physical Description: _____
_____

Family Tree: _____
_____

Background: _____
_____

Weapon: _____

Place of Origin: _____

Known Locations: _____

Companions: _____

Aliases: _____

Associations: _____

Important Life Events: _____
_____

Name: _____
_____

Age: _____

Birthday: _____

Species/Race: _____
_____

Culture: _____
_____
_____
_____

Physical Description: _____
_____

Family Tree: _____
_____

Background: _____
_____

Weapon: _____

Place of Origin: _____

Known Locations: _____

Companions: _____

Aliases: _____

Associations: _____

Important Life Events: _____
_____

B. Plot Points: Keep it Straight

Jot down your general plot outline here—
no need for a novel! Just the facts, ma'am.

Do your characters travel? Sketch out their journey on a rough map! How far is it (in the system you devised to track such measurements)? How long will it take them to get there?

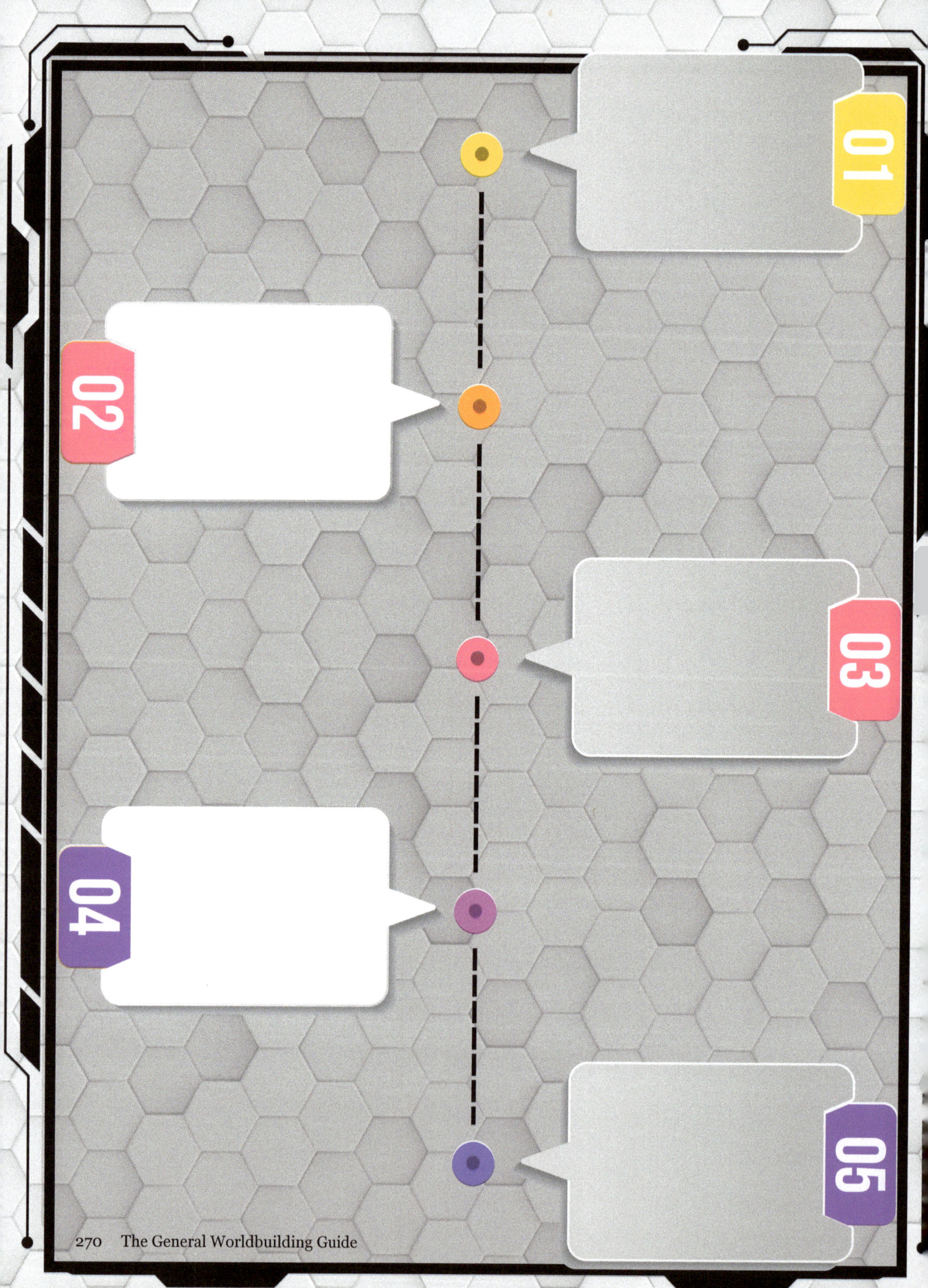

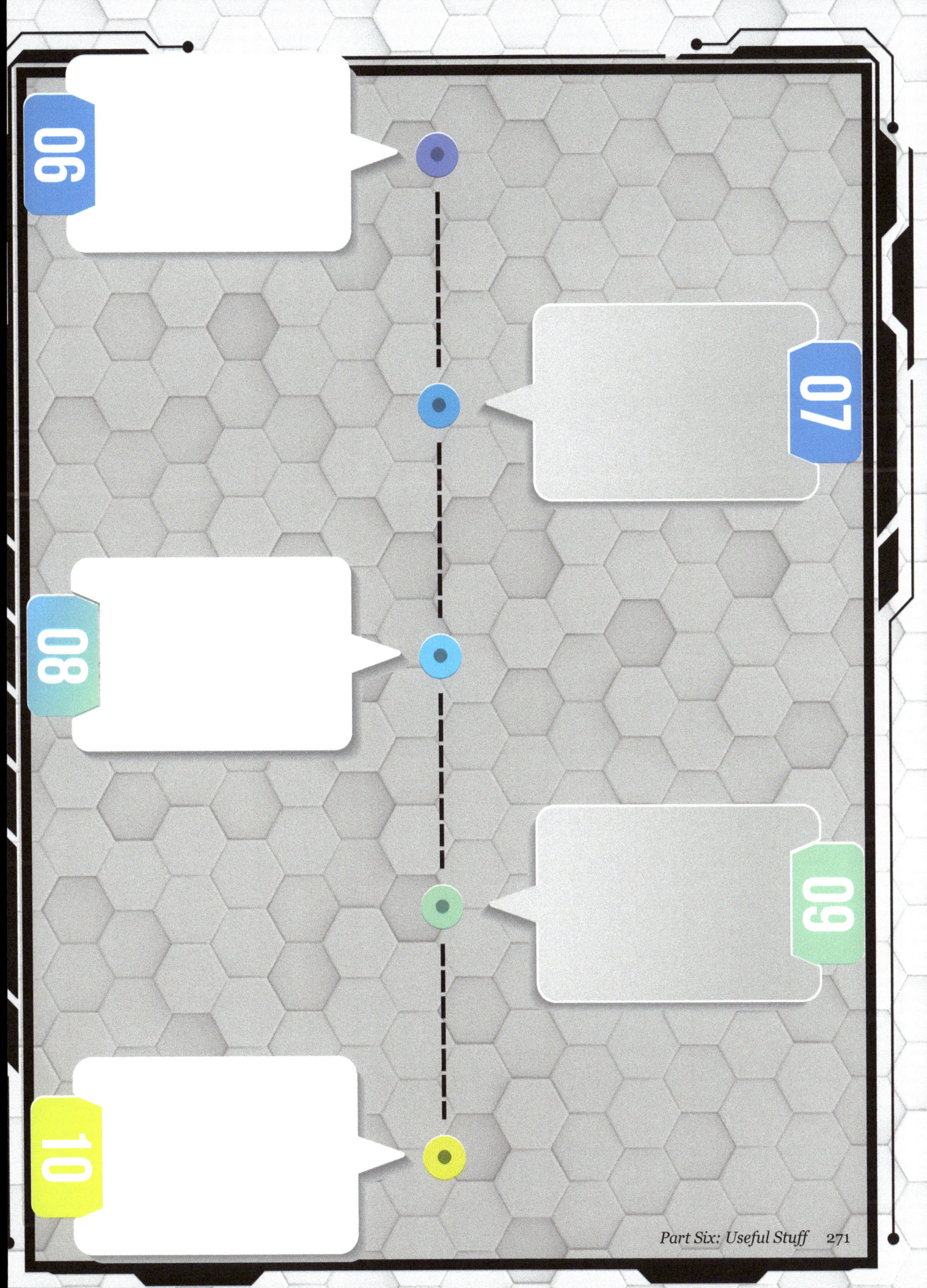

C. Story Profile Time

What genre are you writing?

One sentence summary of the story you are writing:

Why are you the one to write this story?

Why does the world need to read this story?

What makes this story different from all the others like it?
(Hint: you didn't write all those other stories!)

Who will read this story? Describe your target audience.

_____

_____

Keywords that apply to this story:

_____

_____

Format (short story, novella, novel, etc.):

_____

Word count of this story:

_____

Approximate timeline for planning purposes

_____

- Outline (if you do that sort of thing): _____
- First half drafted: _____
- Second half drafted: _____
- Rough draft completed: _____
- First edits completed: _____
- Beta reader round: _____
- Second edits completed: _____
- Ready to send out or publish: _____

D. Top Five Time

Top Tens can be intimidating, so let's stick with the first five things that pop into your mind about your world!

- Top Five songs everyone knows at a bar

_____   _____

_____   _____

_____

- Top Five songs everyone hates to hear (Not that one again!)

_____   _____

_____   _____

_____

- Top Five Works of Art everyone has an opinion about

_____

_____

_____

_____

_____

- Top Five heroes everyone idolizes

  _____   _____

  _____   _____

  _____

- Top Five modes of transportation

  _____   _____

  _____   _____

  _____

- Top Five conspiracy theories

  _____

  _____

  _____

  _____

  _____

Part Six: Useful Stuff

- Top Five books in everyone's house

  _____
  _____
  _____
  _____
  _____

- Top Five things everyone knows about the world

  _____
  _____
  _____
  _____
  _____

- Top Five things everyone thinks about the world (but are totally wrong)

  _____
  _____
  _____
  _____
  _____

- Top Five myths that everyone knows aren't true

  _____
  _____
  _____
  _____
  _____

- Top Five best rulers of all time

- Top Five worst rulers of all time

- Top Five villains everyone secretly loves

- Top Five things parents tell their children

- Top Five ways lovers woo their beloved

- Top Five reasons for relationships to end

Part Six: Useful Stuff

- Top Five favorite foods

  _____   _____
  _____   _____
  _____   _____

- Top Five languages in the world

  _____   _____
  _____   _____
  _____   _____

- Top Five popular fashion choices right now

  _____   _____
  _____   _____
  _____   _____

- Top Five worst fashion trends that everyone despises now

  _____   _____
  _____   _____
  _____   _____

- Top Five reasons your story is freaking awesome

  _____
  _____
  _____
  _____
  _____

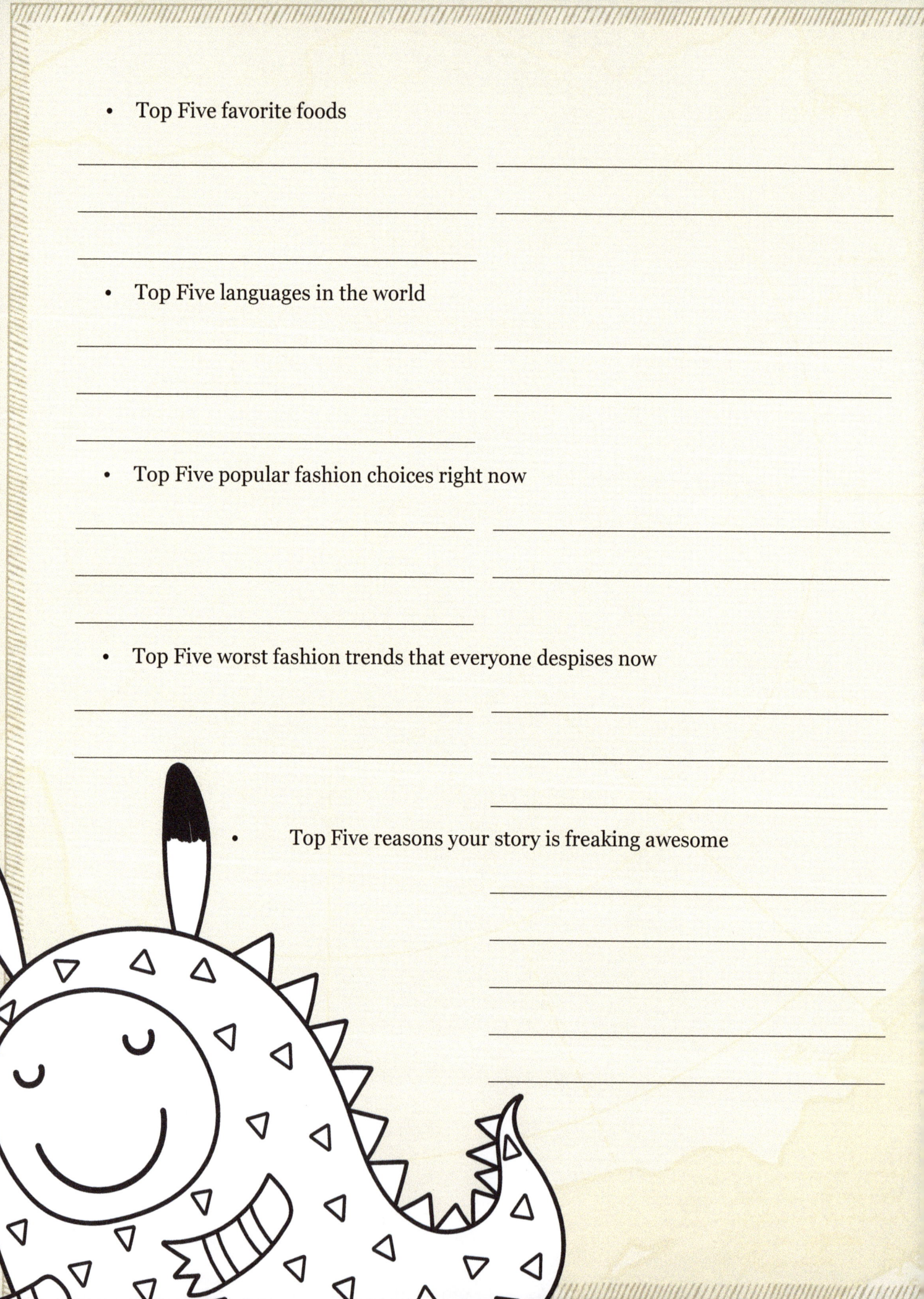

YOU MADE IT!

Time to reward yourself with something nice—and then get to work on that story! You've done the homework; now enjoy the ride.

References mentioned in this book

The 13th Warrior. Dir. John McTiernan. Buena Vista Pictures. 1999.

Aesop's Fables. Ed. GK Chesterton. 2016.

AI. Dir by Steven Spielberg. Warner Bros. 2001.

Ashen, Dominic. *Steel & Thunder*. 4 Horsemen Publications 2021.

Avengers. Marvel Cinematic Universe. 2012-2023.

The Boys. Developed by Eric Kripke. Amazon. 2019+

Bronte, Charlotte. *Jane Eyre*. Smith, Elder, & Co. 1847.

Buffy the Vampire Slayer. Created by Joss Whedon. Mutant Enemy. 1997-2003.

Bulfinch, Thomas. *Bulfinch's Mythology*. Lee and Shepard, 1867.

Campbell, Joseph. *The Hero with a Thousand Faces*. Pantheon. 1949.

Card, Orson Scott. Ender's Game. Tor. 1985-2008.

Carlson, Ty. *The Bench*. 4 Horsemen Publications. 2021.

Cline, Ernest. *Ready Player One*. Crown. 2011.

Coleman, JA. *The Dictionary of Mythology*. Arcturus Publishing. 2007.

Collins, Suzanne. The Hunger Games. Scholastic. 2008-2010.

Deadpool (and *Deadpool* 2). Dir. Tim Miller. Fox. 2016+

DeVivo, Maria. *Witch of the Black Circle*. 4 Horsemen Publications. 2021.

De Worde, Wynken. *A Gest of Robyn Hode*. 1500.

Early Irish Myths and Sagas. Penguin. 1982.

Ellis, Peter Beresford. *The Mammoth Book of Celtic Myths and Legends*. Robinson. 2022.

Erik the Viking. United. 1989.

Freytag, Gustav. *Debit and Credit*. 1857.

Gaiman, Neil. *Norse Mythology*. W.W. Norton and Company, 2017.

Grimm's Fairy Tales. 1812-1858.

Hamilton, Edith. *Mythology*. Little, Brown and Company, 1942.

Herbert, Frank. Dune. Chilton Books. 1965-1985.

Homer. *The Iliad* and *The Odyssey*. (I like Robert Fagles' translation, 1998)

Hugo, Victor. *The Hunchback of Notre Dame*. Gosselin. 1831.

Hugo, Victor. *Les Miserables*. Lacroix, Verboeckhoven & Cie. 1862.

Jordan, Robert. The Wheel of Time. Tor. 1990-2013.

Jupiter Ascending. Dir. The Wachowskis. Warner Bros. 2015.

King, Stephen. The Dark Tower. 1982-2012.

King, Stephen and Peter Straub. *The Talisman*. Viking. 1984.

Lambert, Dee. *Rydan*. 4 Horsemen Publications. 2021.

Lowry, Lois. *The Giver*. Houghton Mifflin, 1993.

Orsino, Danielle. Birth of the Fae. Four Horsemen Publications. 2021-2022.

Ovid. *Metamorphoses*.

Paquette, JM. Conjuring Fascination. 4 Horsemen Publications. 2020-2022

Paquette, JM. *Klauden's Ring*. 4 Horsemen Publications. 2020.

Poetic Edda. various translations since the 13th century.

Pratchett, Terry. Discworld. 1983-2015.

Resident Evil. Dir. Paul Anderson. 2002-2016.

Rick and Morty. Warner Bros. 2006-present.

Riordan, Rick. Percy Jackson. 2005-2009.

Roth, Veronica. Divergent. Harper Collins. 2011-2013.

Rowling, J.K. Harry Potter. 1997-2007.

Saenz, Lyra. *Prelude*. 4 Horsemen Publications. 2021.

Shakespeare, William. *Hamlet*. 1600.

Shrek. DreamWorks. 2001-2010.

Simons, TS. *Antipodes*. 4 Horsemen Publications. 2020.

Star Trek. Created by Gene Roddenberry. 1966+

Star Wars. Created by George Lucas. 1977+

Sturluson, Snorri. *Prose Edda*. ca. 1300.

Tarrant, Mark. *The Mighty Hook*. 4 Horsemen Publications. 2022.

Titan AE. Dir. Don Bluth. Fox. 2000.

Tolkien, J.R.R. *The Legend of Sigurd & Gudrun*. Harper Collins. 2009.

Tolkien, J.R.R. *Lord of the Rings* (also *The Hobbit* and *The Silmarillion*). 1954-1955, 1937, 1977.

Tolkien, J.R.R. "On Fairy Stories." *Essays Presented to Charles Williams*. Oxford UP, 1947.

Tolstoy, Leo. *Anna Karenina*. The Russian Messenger. 1878.

Virgil. *The Aeneid*. Any translation.

Weir, Andy. *The Martian*. Crown. 2014.

Westbrook, CK. *The Shooting*. 4 Horsemen Publications. 2021.

White, TH. *The Once and Future King*. Collins. 1958.

The Witcher. Created by Lauren Schmidt Hissrich. Netflix. 2019+

Wonderdraft. www.wonderdraft.net

Yasuda, Anita. *Sky Woman and the Big Turtle*. Magic Wagon. 2012.

Hey there--what are you doing here? It's over. Go buy another copy if you want to build another world--or check out one of the other versions availabe for your genre!

More books from Accomplishing Innovation Press

Coloring Books

Jenn Kotick
Mermaids

Workbooks

4HP Writer's Resources
The Author's Accountability Planner

The General Worldbuilding Guide
The Science Fiction Worldbuilding Guide
The Paranormal Worldbuilding Guide
The Romance Worldbuilding Guide
The Fantasy Worldbuilding Guide

Jörgen Jensen with Peter Lundgren
Mind Over Tennis: Mastering the Mental Game

Josh Stehle
I Am A Suphero Expert: Growing Up with my Autistic Brother

Kiyomi Holland
HeARTwork

Lael Giebel
Sustainability is for Everyone: Beginning Steps to Creating a Sustainability Program for Your Business

Letitia Washington
The Psychology of Character Building for Authors

Megan Mackie
Advanced Con Quest

N.B. Johnson
Wonders and Miracles

Valerie Willis
Writer's Bane: Research
Writer's Bane: Formatting 101
Writer's Bane: Plot & Foreshadowing
Writer's Bane: Revisions & Edition (w/ JM Paquette)
Writer's Bane: Character Development

Academia & Textbooks

Dr. Jenifer Paquette
Sentence Diagramming 101: Fun with Linguistics (and Movies)

Textbooks
Composition and Grammar: For HCC by HCC

Discover more at Accomplishing Innovation Press

www.ingramcontent.com/pod-product-compliance
Lightning Source LLC
Chambersburg PA
CBHW061110070526
44583CB00027B/3243